Jesus, Where Are You?

GOING THROUGH YOUR SEASONS WITH HOPE

SOPHIA C. TERRELONGE

Jesus, Where Are You?
Going Through Your Seasons With Hope

Copyright ©2020 by Sophia Cameil Terrelonge

Lincross Publishing

ISBN: 978-1-948581-66-0

Interior Design: Erica D. Hearns, By Her Shelf Media LLC

In memory of my mother:
Adlin Pretina Bennett
My first confidant and cheerleader
Sleep on in peace Mommy
We will meet again in heaven.

Contents

Introduction

I never thought I would be a Christian author, although I've been a dedicated Christian since age ten. My initial perception of Jesus Christ was that He would simply bless all of my personal plans.

Until 2016, I strategized how life would play out: I would get several degrees, and then become Dr. Sophia C. Terrelonge. Next, I would become a renowned professor at a reputable university. I would be married to a kind, educated Christian man - of course! We would have four high-achieving, wonderful Christian children. We would all live happily ever after, basking in sunshine and all things good. It was a great plan in my eyes. But was it the will of God for my life?

I started to get inklings that my plans were not aligned with God's will towards the end of my doctoral studies. Was I really supposed to be an Economics professor? I shrugged it off and continued to work hard. I wanted to fulfil all of my plans for my life. Jesus should just bless my goals as they materialized!

I now realize that this was a very idolatrous mindset. I relegated Jesus Christ to the passenger seat, because I wanted to drive my life to my destination. However, Jesus never shares His glory with another. So when my planned agenda stopped working, I panicked. Why wasn't Jesus facilitating my plans? Why wasn't He showing up anymore? Where was Jesus Christ?

What followed was my greatest season of trials to date. This wilderness period covers the last two years of my doctoral programme and the following nineteen months. It started with the promise of a new career, in which I would excel to the glory of God and the good of my family. It descended into the chaos of the American academic and research labor markets. My story reached rock bottom, which (I thought) a hard worker and a "good" Christian should not endure. But God was no longer speaking and moving in the landscape of my life. I would sit and ask, "Jesus, where are You?"

After this season ended and my life regained stability, I just wanted to forget about it. I wanted to hide my perceived failures, so I had decided to not talk about it. I didn't want to write this book. But Jesus had other plans. He did not want me to shelve it; He wanted me to share my story. I wrote for more than a year. Every time I tried to walk away, the Holy Spirit would remind me and encourage me to write again, little by little.

I hope that this book will minister to you in your special circumstance. May you hear Jesus speaking to you as you read these words. May you possess clarity of vision and hearing to accurately discern His instructions in your current season.

Let's pray:

> *Lord Jesus, I pray for the person reading this book. Let them know You are not distant and uncaring. Please send angels in human form to speak words of encouragement and give hugs of Your love and grace. Let this person's heart begin to feel again, to live again, to hear from You again. Let this mind receive peace from all the uncertainty, pain, embarrassment, disappointment and despair. Father, surround them with Your eternal love right now. Lord, please send help for every need, and provide Your healing balm for every wound and every scar. Lord Jesus, whatever I fail to ask of You, I pray that You will grant it unto this person, who is Your beloved. Amen.*

It doesn't matter where you come from, what you've done and your current situation: Jesus loves you. Dearly beloved, receive grace, peace, wisdom and strength right now in Jesus' name. Now let's begin to walk back in time...

Chapter 1
Us Two and Me Alone

"My name is Sophia Terrelonge." Jamaican children are taught to introduce themselves by stating their names with loud confidence. Say which school you attend, where you live, your mother's name (Adlin Pretina Bennett), your father's name (Earl Joseph Terrelonge) and your hobbies. When you're young, revealing yourself is so easy.

I am the product of a single-parent home. Unfortunately, this seems to be the norm for poor children born in my generation. Fathers were either missing in action, present but absent, or dead. Jamaican mothers tend to play both parental roles and struggle to keep life together for their children. They strive through prayers, tears and tons of sweat to push their children to a better life.

I was the last of seven children for my mother, and I was born in Kingston, Jamaica. Just before my sixth birthday, I lost my brother Leslie Thomas to murder. A few months after that birthday, I also lost my sister Susan Terrelonge to a long illness. After these traumatic deaths, my father, mother, paternal grandmother and I lived for a few years in my father's village in the St. Andrew hills. Life was very difficult and made worse by my father restricting us from socializing with others. My father was verbally abusive and often threatened violence, so my mother decided to leave him. Their relationship lasted about sixteen years. When I was ten, my mother and I moved to the farming community of Darliston, Westmoreland, where we lived with my mother's father, Pappy (Ernest Bennett). We lived so far from the main road that we really didn't live in Darliston - we lived at the foot of Mount Blessed. However, I was happier there alone with my mother. I had friends from school and I enjoyed my childhood in Westmoreland.

Bishop Baron Higgins of the Darliston Christ Gospel Apostolic Church was instrumental in leading us to Jesus Christ. When we met Bishop Higgins, he was in his mid-seventies. He would walk all over Darliston to conduct prayers and invite people to church. He would walk to our house at least once per week. I would hear him calling us outside in the early morning dew, as he strove to catch us at home to tell us about Jesus. He was a true Christ ambassador. After about two months of these visits, we visited the church. We then became regular church attendees. My mother and I accepted Jesus as our Lord and Savior in 1995. We were baptized on March 19, 1995 and received the gift of the Holy Spirit on April 2, 1996.[1] I often think of my mother and I, as the inseparable twins: "us two".

My father visited us a few times in Darliston as he hoped to reconcile with my mother. But she was happy with Jesus alone. He soon ceased all communications with us in spite of my many written letters. So, we left him to his solitude.

My mother toiled as a domestic worker on select weekdays for different families. I was angry that she had to wash people's dirty clothes for our survival. Back then, I secretly hated everyone she worked for. They didn't pay her enough to wash all their household laundry *by hand* and then clean their homes afterwards.

I was a guilty and depressed teenager and I contemplated suicide several times. I thought that if I died, then my mother wouldn't need to work so hard. She would only need to focus on herself and Pappy since all her other surviving children were adults. I once asked her how she would feel if I was dead. Mommy quickly discerned that I was struggling with suicidal thoughts. Out came the tried-and-proven "mother's guilt": I would be heartless to let her suffer from losing more children. What about the stories people would devise to explain why I killed myself? Why would I give her such stress in her old age? Wasn't

---

1 Please read Acts 2 for context.

it she who had me? I just needed to be "a good" (meaning "a not promiscuous") girl, study my books very well and come out to "pass the worst."[2] So I became a "good" girl. I was "perfect" for everyone outside our "us two". No one else knew about my suicidal tendencies.

We ate *chicken back*[3] in a number of ways. Each meal would be cooked in the oil obtained from frying the fat from said chicken back. I learned how to eat boiled breadfruit and boiled green bananas. My staple shifted from my favorite, rice, to ground provisions grown at home - yam, dasheen and coco.[4]

In my teen years I got as rotund as my mother due to this high-carb diet. Unfortunately, this drew the eyes, voices and hands of men (young, old, unmarried and married) as they gave me the attention I feared and hated. I believed that all men were evil, sent from the devil to make me pregnant and then forever poor like my mother. Everyone with a penis was a potential pervert, a rapist and a killer of my dreams. These dreams of no longer having to use pit latrine or take my "showers" using buckets of water in an outside bath house. My dreams also included possessing far more clothes and shoes, and eating "proper" food

2 "Pass the worst", means becoming a self-sufficient adult.
3 Chicken is expensive in Jamaica, but the chicken back (that is, the chicken's backbone and its immediate connections) is an affordable alternative. We refer to chicken back as "poor man's steak".
4 Yam, dasheen and coco are edible Jamaican tubers.

every day. I was driven to escape this existence via a good education.

I am very grateful to Jesus Christ that I did not pay a single cent of tuition fees for all my degrees. God provided a full scholarship every single step of the way. Thank you Jesus! Hallelujah! ☺ Back then; this testimony was unimaginable.

I completed my CSECs (formerly CXCs) and GCEs[5] with the best grades from the little but tallawah[6] Maud McLeod High School. The payments of my exam fees were difficult for Mommy, but by God's grace she made them. Upon the recommendation of Ms. D. - an exceptional teacher and ardent financial supporter - I did my GCE A' Levels[7] at the Manning's School in Savanna-la-mar.

In 2002, I got into my dream university: The University of the West Indies at Mona, Jamaica (UWI, Mona). I studied my Bachelor of Science degree in Economics and Management Studies. My dear mother could only afford to send me J$1000 per week (or US$21 back then). So I worked on campus to cover accommodation and food, as my scholarship only covered my tuition. I never purchased

5 CSECs and GCEs are the Caribbean's equivalent of a GED in the USA or a high school diploma.
6 "Tallawah" means to be strong-willed and resilient.
7 GCE Advanced Levels (A' Levels) are formal exams taken in order to be accepted into certain three-year universities in the Caribbean region. Now we have CAPE exams that serve that purpose as well.

text books - I relied on the library resources. I got my first job working in the baggage area of the library. I asked Mommy not to send the J$1000 each week, as I could now manage. She adjusted to sending the J$1000 every two weeks or so. I spent my nights poring over books. This eventually took a toll on my eyes, as I now wear glasses.

After three years, I graduated with First Class Honors much to the delight of my mother who proudly attended my UWI graduation. Upon the recommendation of a professor, I began my Master of Science in Economics in 2005. My tuition fees were waived, as I worked as a teaching assistant and a research assistant in my department. I was happy to receive my J$20,000 per month (about US$320 then) as my stipend. I also worked as a proctor (or invigilator) for the undergraduate final exams at UWI. My mother was now able to keep her money for herself. I had "passed the worst".

After my Master of Science degree, I worked as an Assistant Lecturer for two years. This period allowed us to determine if we wanted to remain in academia - which meant going overseas for further doctoral studies. But if we discovered that we didn't like teaching so much, then we would go into the private/public sectors to fill economist positions. It was at the beginning of this stint that our crisis began.

At the end of my second degree, Mommy complained of a lump under her left armpit. I repeatedly asked her to seek medical attention. But since I didn't have enough to pay for this visit, she didn't go (plus she hated hospitals). Once I got my pay check from being a full-time Assistant Lecturer, I booked a doctor's visit. She had the time available, because I had stopped her from working. She went, but in typical Jamaican fashion, we got the run-around of continual visits. They eventually biopsied the growing lump and found it was cancer.

My mother had surgery to remove her left breast in March 2008. She received oral chemotherapy, but she was scared to do radiation treatment. A close relative had undergone radiation treatments and the result was blackened body parts. We focused on healthy eating and natural juices, removing stress and having someone to help her at home. She was still independent and insisted on caring for Pappy. I drove from Kingston to Westmoreland every other weekend to do her shopping and make sure that she was funded and comfortable.

I hoped that she would fully recover. Her surgery wound had healed well. She had edema in her left arm, but exercise eventually shrunk it. Then my grandfather Pappy died in October 2008. My mother was deeply saddened, and I noticed a sudden decline. Our foreign-based relatives chose to bury my grandfather on November 1st, my mother's birthday. I asked her why she didn't tell them not to bury Pappy on her birthday. In her characteristic calm way, she said that she didn't mind and that she just wanted him to be buried in peace. That birthday would be the last one that I would spend with my beloved mother.

The lumps returned more aggressively. She had the second surgery in January 2009, and was noticeably weaker afterwards. I moved her to live with me in Kingston until the end of May 2009. During that time, I took her to Barbados - her first and only plane trip - for a vacation. We even went to get her US visa. She was so proud of herself that she was able to go into the big US Embassy, speak to the Embassy personnel, and get her visa. But she would never see the America that she always wanted to visit.

We went through hell. In her last month of living with me, she developed a hard rock-like substance that first covered her entire left side. She began to eat less, and became irritable when we coaxed her to eat more. She cried at nights from the pain. I couldn't sleep, she couldn't sleep. I think that's one of the reasons she requested to go back home in May 2009. Mommy knew that she was dying. This rock slowly encircled my mother's middle section in an unforgiving armor. It reduced her to only eating porridge, drinking liquids and being bed-ridden.

I moved her back to Westmoreland as she requested. In June 2009, I sat in the doctor's office at the Savanna-la-mar hospital. The doctor firmly told me that she would die - we had at most three months. When I came out of his office, my mother looked at my face and asked me outright if the doctor said she would die. I could only nod my head in assent. My older brother Byron (now deceased) lived with her in Westmoreland as I continued to work at UWI. I now made the eight-hour round trip to Westmoreland every weekend. Between my eldest brother Byron and my second oldest sister Marla (Gloria), my mother was cared for and taken for her doctor's visits. My other sister Jewell and brother Robert would also call and visit her, as they lived further away.

Mommy was prescribed stronger doses of morphine, but she hated it. Although she felt no pain, morphine made her mentally vague. Mommy liked being in control of herself and her environment. She became understandably moody and querulous. She often prayed aloud to Jesus Christ to take her home. At first, I didn't want her to die. But when I saw how much she was suffering, my prayers changed from "Jesus, please heal my mother" to "God, why can't you listen to my mother and take her home? Please let her stop suffering!"

My mother was admitted to the Savanna-la-mar hospital for the last time on Thursday July 30, 2009. I finished my last day of work at UWI on Friday July 31st. I would begin my Ph.D. in Economics at the State University of New York (SUNY) at Binghamton in August 2009. Mommy wanted me to be occupied after her death to lessen the impact on me. She knew that I would fly to the USA on August 7, 2009. She kept saying: "I wish I could die, so that you could just bury me and then go off to study."

God granted her wish. I went to Westmoreland on August 1st and went straight to visit her in the hospital. We kept visiting the hospital. Jesus granted my mother the chance to make peace with Him and everyone else before she died. On the evening of Monday August 3, 2009, my mother died. I like to think that she died with a clean heart and a pure conscience. She was finally free from the pain and cares of life. She was 68 years of age.

She never got to see her 69th birthday. Her last birthday was not one of celebration, but one of mourning at her father's funeral. Mommy died of carcinoma in situ. The cancer had spread all over her body and calcified her liver. It became rock-hard and trapped her in that internal armor.

I delayed my departure and sprang into funeral-planning mode. We buried my mother on Sunday August 16, 2009 and three days later I was in Binghamton, NY. I was in a new place, ready to start a new phase of my life, while still grieving the abrupt end of her life. I was now alone. I had no confidant and cheerleader on earth anymore. "Us two" had become "me alone". I would become my own cheerleader and Jesus Christ became my sole confidant.

Afterthoughts

I still grieve my mother's passing. I also grieve the loss of my siblings and other family members. However, the pain in my heart lessens with each passing year. I pray that you receive the peace and comfort of Jesus Christ in your time of bereavement. I pray that you will be able to remember the great moments with your loved ones and the insightful lessons you gleaned from them. Live your life in full accordance with God's will. Live, laugh, love and thrive: if they were still here, they would want you to do so. Remember that Jesus loves you and He rejoices over you with singing,[8] because you are His beloved.

---

8 Zephaniah 3:17.

Chapter 2
Relocation: Moving on Up! New Life!

On my fourth day in New York, I was in a new graduate students' meet-and-greet session. I met with my cohort, older cohorts and my new professors at the State University of New York (SUNY) at Binghamton. My doctoral studies and a new chapter of my life had begun.

I had promised my mother in her latter days that I would be stronger, wiser, take good care of myself here on earth and meet her in heaven. I would often think to call my mother to update her. But each time, the bitter memory of her death would shock me back to reality.

I intensely mourned my mother for a year. Every morning I would lie in bed and repeat: "My mother is dead. Mommy is dead." Invariably hot tears would spring to my eyes. Sometimes I would have a cry, other times, the tears would dry quicker. One evening I was on the campus shuttle returning from school. As I looked out the window and over the Chenango River, a thought struck me. My love for my mother was so vast that I would never stop grieving her loss. I would only be able to grieve for her in parts over the years. So I made peace with my inner sadness and soldiered on.

I applied to SUNY Binghamton with the "head knowledge" that it wasn't in New York City (NYC), but with the "heart feeling" that it would be like NYC. Boy was I wrong! I remember seeing all the "board" (wooden) single-family houses on my way from the airport. I wondered why they had these board houses[9] which I equated with poverty. Why was this place looking so much like "country"? What kind of "bush place"[10] was this? I was very disappointed.

After staying for a week with another Jamaican grad student, I moved into my first apartment on Carhart Avenue. I had my own bedroom, but shared everything else with two roommates - one straight from China and an American-born Chinese (ABC). There were interesting differences between the women. The Chinese lady had a rice cooker and she was fascinated whenever I cooked rice in a pot. For me it was great that I had an electric stove to

---

9 Some of these houses were actually clad in an aluminum siding that resembled wooden planks.

10 Jamaican rural areas are characterized by many trees and a few small buildings. Jamaicans refer to these areas as "country" or less euphemistically: "bush".

cook on instead of scorching my respiratory system over a fireside[11] like I did in my youth. On the other hand, the ABC lady ate-out most of the times and kept to herself.

My first-time seeing snow was magical! It fell in beautiful powdery clusters from the sky to lie along the road, on the faded grass, on the tree limbs and on the cars. Delightful white fluffiness was everywhere! I walked carefully on it with my new winter boots. The wonder started to slip away once I got to the main street to wait on my campus shuttle. I realized that when a lot of people walked in the snow, it lost its pristine quality and became a dirty muck. I then discovered that snow turns to ice. The bus was late and I was slowly freezing to death because I didn't wear enough layers. The cold increased my urge to pee, but I was stuck. I couldn't go back to the house, miss the bus and be late! As an answer to my increasingly frantic prayers pushed out on misty breaths, the bus came. I rushed aboard into the warmth!

A pro tip to renting in a temperate climate is to ensure that heat is included. We got a US$300 gas heating bill

---

11 A fireside was a raised concrete platform with spaces to create small fires. Each fire space had three large stones on which to position a cooking pot. You added more wood to the fire to increase the heat. You withdrew wood pieces (or "draw" the fire) to reduce the heat. You would often bend close to the fire to blow it into a blaze, or use a flat object (cardboard, old plastic lid, etc.) to fan the flames to burn brighter.

in January 2010 when we were using electric heaters and hiding under blankets the whole time! The furnace was not working and our Chinese landlords didn't care to do anything other than their unofficial tinkering on the device. The ABC lady broke lease first, followed by the Chinese lady. I was left alone in a freezing flat. Thankfully the landlords agreed to move me to their next property (also their home) at Schubert Street, which was carpeted and warm. I lived on the second floor with two Caucasian roommates.

Unfortunately, these two young women were simply untidy. Their discarded hair strands often clogged the shower, and they believed in the existence of an invisible kitchen fairy. I was miserable. When I spoke to them about cleaning up after themselves, they went passive aggressive and got infinitely worse. The fridge was a minefield and I became paranoid about them messing with my food. Thus, I kept everything sealed or specially tied in a confusing, Jamaican-Granny fashion to be tamper-proof. I suffered through the remaining months of the second semester.

I was done with having roommates. After all, I was a 26-year-old woman who had no time to deal with the vagaries of other persons on top of grad school pressures. I wanted to live alone. I got a one-bedroom apartment right on Main Street Binghamton, where the water-based heat was included in the rent. I also had a nice furnished kitchen all to myself! I bought second-hand furniture and Walmart plastic shelving units to organize my bedroom and living room to my taste. I loved that little apartment and liked the landlord so much, that I stayed there until after my graduation in 2015.

Life in upstate NY was both idyllic and frantic. The landscape was peaceful and didn't jar me mentally. This was a Godsend, as grad school often made me think that I was going insane! The first hurdle was adjusting to being a student again after two years. I was no longer the teacher instructing the class. I had to listen and absorb the course content, and then apply the knowledge to complete assignments, write papers and do exams. That transition from full-time lecturer to full-time student took about two semesters. However, by the grace of God I made it through my first year courses pretty well.

Everyone back home in Jamaica thought I lived in NYC. I always told them I lived about three hours away (via bus) from NYC. I didn't live anywhere that looked like NYC. I lived in the "bush-bush"[12] upstate region in *NY State*. However, I did find time to explore NYC, traveling bravely by the MTA train system and taking the ferry over

---

12 In Jamaica we repeat words to give emphasis. Therefore "bush-bush" would be "a deeply rural area". ☺

to Staten Island to explore. I mainly stuck to NY State - except when I went to conferences in other states. Perhaps I should have spent more time exploring the USA while I had the chance.

My time in grad school was a period of growth in the educational, social and spiritual spheres. I soon became a pretty solid student in the Economics Ph.D. program. It was a boon to my department that I taught before in higher education. So, I quickly moved from being a teaching assistant to an adjunct instructor teaching my own classes. I made friends with my fellow grad students from different cultures. They were often amazed that I would know so much about their culture when each of them was my first personal contact with the same. I would tell them that I was secretly an anthropologist who made it her life's mission to study other cultures.

I also attended church regularly. I started out with a very-little-tongue-talking, predominantly white, large-congregation church. However, I began to feel the need for something more familiar, more like Jamaica. I then joined a majority-black church where I felt more connected. At that church the small congregation was mainly Black American with some Guyanese, Trinidadian and Jamaican thrown in for good measure. It was there that I learned about praise breaks and a lot about the Black American church.

My ultimate expectations were still on track; the way that my life was "supposed" to play out in America. I had passed all my comprehensive exams in the spring 2011 semester and I was writing my dissertation. Everything seemed set for a spring 2014 graduation and a launch into an academic career in the US. All was aligned - it was all going to plan as per my agenda. However it was also around this time (in 2012) that I was really seeking Jesus. I was going deeper into His Word and asking Jesus about His will for my life. I remember one late night worship session in my apartment when I was singing Hillsong United's *Oceans*.

I was really immersed in the song and worshipping Jesus, when I heard His Holy Spirit ask me: "Do you really mean what you're singing?"

I responded in my mind: "Yes Jesus! I will follow You wherever You lead me!"

The Holy Spirit asked me again: "Do you really mean that?"

I was emphatic with tears flowing down my face: "Yes Jesus! Yes! I will go into the unknown with You!"

I heard Him ask me: "Are you sure?"

"Yes, Jesus! Yes!"

"Ok."

My life was irrevocably changed from that point (although I didn't realize it then). I made a covenant with Jesus Christ that night. I agreed to surrender my will to His will. I'm now really wary about that song! ☺ It's nice when God's will match our expectations about our life paths. However what happens when Jesus leads us into oceans unknown, into unexpected tempests? Do we believe that negative occurrences are all a part of His plan for our lives? What do we do when we perceive that Jesus is about to exit stage-left out of our lives? I was about to find out.

Afterthoughts

Expectations: we all tend to have them about ourselves, other people, places and things. We are delighted when reality exceeds what we expect. On the flip side when reality doesn't align with what we expect, we often plunge into despair. At times, we cannot avoid having some expectations. However, it's important to also remember that reality can be either more or less than those ideals. We must keep our emotions on an even keel to avoid continually swinging from one extreme emotion to the next. You have to know how to "balance and steady" throughout life's motions.

We live in a multicultural society. Globalization has ensured that even the most racial and culturally homogenized countries are now exposed to other cultures. Although I had studied other cultures from afar, it was a totally different thing when I was living in close proximity to that same culture. I had to learn how to engage with other cultures with a view to accepting our differences and enjoying our similarities. I also had to learn (and I am still learning) how to accept another person's habits even when I do not like them. It is the Jamaican ethos of "live and let live". The Word even advises us to do all that we can to "live peaceably" with everyone that we meet.[13] So just live in peace and harmony with all.

---

13 Romans 12:18.

Chapter 3

Job Market!
Job Market!

In the land of Academia, we have an annual "job market".[14] This job market is like a massive dating service. Universities, companies and soon-to-be-minted PhDs all come together to find the perfect match. It's speed dating on steroids - but for academics! All economists converge on the city hosting the AEA's ASSA[15] conference every January. I was ecstatic to attend my first job market in Philadelphia, PA. I worked very hard in grad school, and it was now my fifth year. I was all fasted-up[16] and prayed-up for success! I was in very high spirits!

The academic job market is serious business, as its

---

14 In reality, it is more like a job fair. However I will use the terminology familiar to social sciences academia.

15 AEA means American Economic Association, while ASSA means Allied Social Sciences Associations.

16 Fasting means to refrain from eating and drinking for a period of time. This can be for a few hours, a day, or days as led by the Holy Spirit. This empowers a child of God to give precedence to spiritually pursuing Jesus Christ and His will.

preparation period begins the previous September or fall semester. Grad students craft cover letters and CVs, and apply for the posts advertised on dedicated websites. There are letters of glowing recommendation about your research, teaching and overall goodness from all your dissertation committee members. Your research and teaching statements are prepared. Your job market research paper must be perfect. Above all, you need to show why you are the best candidate in an ocean of equally (or more) well-endowed grad students.

I was advised that certain schools (universities and colleges) were out of my reach. It was not because I was a black female foreigner, but because SUNY Binghamton did not have the appropriate rank. There is a totem pole that everyone keeps in place. Ivy League universities hire their own graduates; their job market is in the stratosphere where mere mortals dare not tread. The remaining universities are arranged into divisions and behave like their "betters". SUNY Binghamton was ranked around 98th at that time. Therefore, I could only apply for posts at schools ranked lower than SUNY Binghamton. I had to stay in my lane. As a Jamaican, I decided to still apply for some of the Ivy League university posts. They didn't even condescend to send me a rejection letter. I imagine that my applications gave comic relief to the job search committees[17] in those exalted halls.

I was full of energy and motivated to whittle down my list of job applications. I focused on academia, as I believed that I was a budding academic. I never thought to apply for non-academic jobs. I was intent to get on that tenure-track: first Assistant Professor, then Associate Professor, then fully tenured Professor. I had a goal in sight and I was feverishly working towards it. I didn't even entertain the possibility of failure. I maintained this mindset even as my energy waned and the advertised posts came to a sputtering end. I entered the November Thanksgiving blues, waiting for universities to contact me about scheduling job interviews for the January 2014 conference. By December 2013, I had ten interviews scheduled. I was happy and effervescent. I was sure that at least one university would give me a solid job offer.

I purchased two pants suits and two pairs of sturdy but fashionable boots. I groomed my shoulder-length locks into a mix of cornrows and a neat bun. I ensured that everything was professional: from my look to my speech. I rehearsed in my head all the time. I imagined the questions from the interview panel of each school. I answered their

---

17 A job search committee consists of key faculty members in an academic department. This team is responsible for screening applications for their department's vacancies. They also interview these candidates at the annual AEA-ASSA meetings.

imaginary questions to the best of my ability.

I went to the bus station the day before the AEA conference began. The snow fell the night before and the skies were clear when I left Binghamton. The bus originated from Syracuse and it had to navigate south along the snow-bound roads. We had a late departure by nearly two hours. And as we got closer to Philadelphia, a snow storm brewed.

While I was on the bus I heard a voice reciting Psalm 127:1:

> *"Unless the Lord builds the house,*
> *They labor in vain who build it;*
> *Unless the Lord guards the city,*
> *The watchman stays awake in vain."*

I was disturbed in my spirit. What was this? Failure before I even started? I was confused about this message from God. It was against my belief in getting a US academic job. At the time I even thought that it was coming from the enemy! I put it at the back of my mind: "There was no way God would let me fail!"

It was totally dark once I arrived at the Philadelphia bus station. This was a new city for me. It wasn't as big as NYC, but the oppressive darkness was menacing. The snowfall made the taxis scarce. Every taxi I asked to take me to my hotel refused for a variety of reasons. I was beginning to feel the cold seep into my boots and my hands. My distress steadily increased.

I started to walk up Philadelphia's main thoroughfare in the dark stillness. The snow got deeper as I slowly trudged through a white knee-high obstacle course. I was struggling with my backpack and heavy suitcase. I felt cold to my very bones, my fingers went numb and the suitcase repeatedly fell from my hands. I became frightened and began to cry, but my tears froze on my face. My breath formed a ghostly mist in the night. I breathed in harsh cold and exhaled my remaining warmth. I also felt my bladder fill up. I was lost in a sea of white, in an unfamiliar city, with no one to help me. I thought that I would die from hypothermia and my body would be found in the city streets. I was distraught. I kept praying to Jesus to send someone to help me.

After a while I registered that someone across the street was trying to get my attention through the howling wind. This person was big and tall, and his winter coat made him seem even bigger. The gentleman came across the street and asked me where I was going. I told him the name of the hotel and that I was in Philadelphia to attend the conference. I then learned that I needed to make a left turn further down the street.

I crossed back over the street with him carrying my suitcase, and me still with my backpack. We started towards the adjoining street turn-off. This street ran underneath a poorly-lit bridge that formed a part of an overhead highway. This man sounded nice enough, but I was still wary, as I could not see his face fully due to his head gear and his scarf. I was talking to him, but in my head, I was trying to decide my course of action if he tried to attack me. I didn't care if he took my suitcase; I just cared about my safety.

We eventually got to my hotel. He came with me into the lobby and explained to them that I had gotten lost. The two front desk staff expressed their sympathies. I turned and thanked him profusely with a lot of "God-bless-you" on top. He then left the hotel. After making use of the lobby's restroom, I went up to my room; fell to my knees and thanked God for not letting me die in Philadelphia's snow-covered streets. I cleaned up and fell into an exhausted sleep.

The next morning came too early, as I was still groggy. But I had to wake up and perk up because my first interview was inexpertly set for 8:00 AM. The interviews passed by: some were great, some were bad and some were in-between. I tried to enjoy what I could of Philadelphia in winter. Most of my attention and energy were consumed with worrying before each interview. I worried again as I conducted their post-mortems: my in-depth analyses of all that had occurred with the interview panels. I was a nervous wreck; my head and stomach were out of whack.

I traveled back to Binghamton to await the news of any fly-outs. Fly-outs are the second stage interviews which require traveling to meet key members of the prospective university's department and governance. Most importantly I would present my job market paper at each fly-out. I waited. I waited through my cohort receiving their fly-out notifications. I waited in vain. Out of the ten interviews, I had zero fly-outs! Not a single university wanted to see me again. I was ashamed, heart-broken and depressed.

I applied for the secondary job market, but with no success. I had failed the US academic job market despite my best efforts. Almost all members of my cohort were signing job contracts and here I was, empty. I was nothing. I felt numb. I didn't want to go to school anymore, to face the gushing of faculty, staff and other grad students about the successes of my peers. I didn't want to experience their looks of pity and hushed conversations, as they wondered what was wrong with me. It was unheard of. Usually in my department everyone got a job - even if it was just for a year. I was stranded. I felt alone and I felt a rising resentment against God. Why was I even serving Him anyways? I began to have a crisis of faith, which would only escalate.

Some of my fellow Jamaicans tried to console me, but I still felt like a loser. My dissertation advisor encouraged me to try again the following year, January 2015. This would mean defending my dissertation in my 6th year and not in my 5th year as planned. I was worried that I would be deemed less smart to not have finished my PhD in 5 years. She was confident that something would change in my favor if I tried again. I agreed with her. My teaching assistantship funding was also extended by a year. I decided to try again, to hope again. Anything's still possible, right?

Afterthoughts

Wow! It is really difficult to re-visit my first job market experience. It's sad that I thought that my self-worth as a human being was determined by whether or not I secured an academic job. At the time, the goal of becoming a Professor consumed me to my core. I couldn't even conceive of being anything else but a Professor.

Beloved, never allow your self-worth to be determined by what other people think, say or do! Your worth in this earth is determined by Jesus Christ alone! Do not let your past or your present limit your future. You are unique and you will never be a carbon copy of anyone else! You are special in the eyes of Christ and that's all there is to it! As we say in Jamaica: "Argument done!"[18]

It's usually in hindsight that we get a glimmer of how Jesus has been re-routing our lives all along. Do not fear this re-routing process; it's just Jesus aligning your life to match His lovingly-designed blueprint. Beloved, it's scary when you are in the middle of being re-routed, but trust God. Trust Him that when it's all over, you will be just where Jesus wants you to be: in the middle of His divine will.

---

18 "Argument done" signifies the resolution of all previous disputes.

Chapter 4

Renewed Drive: Anything's Still Possible, Right?

I entered the job market all over again! I revised all of my documents, and watched the job ads like a hawk, ready (but emotionally drained) to make applications. I fasted and prayed a lot for this last-ditch attempt to complete my Ph.D. with a job in hand.

I became paranoid. The first time I entered the job market, I shared freely about my interviews. Now I was brusque and refused to tell anyone about them – not even my dissertation advisor. I was just worried about jinxing my final chance. I was doing all that I could to isolate myself. I put all my energy in this one goal: get an academic job.

I got eight interviews for the AEA 2015 conference in Boston, MA. In the department, I was talked about in hushed tones. People left me alone in my gloomy weirdness. I had an uneventful trip into Boston; no blizzards lurked to freeze me to death, and I found my hotel easily on foot. I packed light and had all my interviews, some were great and others were ok. I was more relaxed and conversational with the interviewers, which made the interviewing panels feel at ease.

I came back home to Binghamton and half-heartedly waited for my fly-out notifications. Again, this second batch was getting calls for fly-outs all over, and all the professors congratulated them. I became almost invisible, but my dissertation advisor was quietly supportive and allowed me to process in silence. She only talked about my papers and upcoming dissertation defense.

And then it happened: I got a fly-out to a private college in Pennsylvania! I was so ecstatic! I had prayed for just one fly-out that would result in a job. This had to be Jesus! Hallelujah!

The college was in a small town, but I was not deterred. I was used to the country life anyways, so I thought that I would be fine. I even began looking at apartments for rent and imagining myself living there.

I told no one about this solitary fly-out. As far as they were concerned, I had no calls once again. I did not want to tell them about it, only to fail and have to deal with their sympathy and/or condescension again. I prepared for it all by myself.

I took a bus from Binghamton, NY to Buffalo, NY, and then the college's driver picked me up and drove me into their town. He was an affable white male in his early fifties, who liked biking and was all about family. We got on very well. I took this as a great sign.

When I drove into town, I discovered that it was tiny, very remote and surrounded by agricultural areas. My driver dropped me off at a small, yet charming bed-and-breakfast. I got there early in the afternoon and prepared for my first meeting - a dinner "date" with two faculty members.

The two gentlemen arrived and took me to a family-owned restaurant for dinner. I ate and talked with them. They answered my queries and I found it was a good interactive atmosphere. Afterwards, they drove me around the town to see various rental apartments, a farmer's market and the doctors' offices, before dropping me back at the bed-and-breakfast. I thanked them and went inside.

I slept well that night in my old-fashioned but cozy bedroom. I woke up and got ready for the long day ahead. I was picked up and taken to meet several college administrators and department personnel. I had insightful conversations where I clearly showed how I would fit in the vision of the college and the activities of the department. I was professionally warm and portrayed myself well.

I had mainly undergrad students and administrative staff at my research presentation. This was a predominantly white small town with most of the students coming from privileged backgrounds. There were few people of color. However since most of the economists were absent, I had to explain a bit more than desired, taking too much time. When I noticed eyes glazing over, I took the hint and concluded my presentation. I had a few questions which I answered and it was all done. I then had lunch with some of the third- and fourth-year students in their dining hall.

I went back to the department's office to process the refund of my round-trip bus ticket and applicable expenses. I then gave the usual goodbyes to the available persons in the department, and was soon bundled off with the assurance that they would get back to me with the results of their job search.

The trip from that little town to Buffalo seemed shorter. I battled a migraine that set in after all excitement from meeting so many strangers. My driver was understanding and pleasant. I bid him goodbye at the Buffalo bus station and went in to the warmth to wait for my bus to Binghamton. We drove along in the icy night towards Binghamton. The snow was falling lightly, as I sat alone in my row of seats in a near empty bus. As I looked into the night, I heard a voice similar to that from the previous year:

"This job will leave you, but it will come back to you."

Jesus, what is this again? Have I not suffered through a failed job search already? When will it be my time to shine? I am from a poor background; I am from a developing country! Why will You not help me to become better in this land of opportunity? I was hurt and I fell into a depressed state from that point.

I waited one week, two weeks, four weeks; nothing came from the college, not a single word. I eventually reached out to the head of the search committee via email in the sixth week. They had gone with another candidate. What? So, none of you people had the decency to let me know before now? I thanked him for the information and went on as best as I could with my life. I didn't even bother with the secondary job market this time. I sent out only a few applications at the bidding of my dissertation supervisor. I was tired of academia and decided to rather pursue an industry or a non-academic job.

I didn't even care anymore. I didn't care that everyone in my department thought of me as a second-time loser. I was bitter and I stopped caring. I just wanted to leave SUNY Binghamton. I was tired of holding out for an elusive academic job that would never come. I re-focused my energy on my new resolution: just graduate!

Afterthoughts

It was hard to relive the deep sense of failure and depression. However, I learned a valuable lesson: Never try to force the will of God. It will never work! Here I was trying to guilt-trip Jesus into giving me an academic job. It's crazy and even blasphemous that I believed I could "make" Jesus do anything! Lord Jesus, I repent of those instances.

Beloved, beware of trying to "block" Jesus in to a corner-He won't play along! He is Sovereign, He can never be contained and His will is the only thing that He will perform! Don't worry; the blueprint that Jesus has for you is the best plan ever for your life! No one - not even you-can make improvements to it. Simply trust Jesus. Know that when He finishes realigning you in His perfect will, it will be good and you will be satisfied. ☺

Chapter 5
The Resolution

My eyes were fixed on the goal: complete my Ph.D. A seventh year in the program wasn't an option! I thought that it was bad enough that I didn't graduate in my fifth year as planned. The additional year was all the damage I would do to my degree. I thought: Who would hire anyone who spent two extra years doing her Ph.D.? They would surely deem me inept and deficient! And besides, I was sick and tired of being a graduate student - I just wanted to leave!

I put the finishing touches on my papers, after including the input of my dissertation committee members. I booked my defense date and then crafted my presentation slides for the day.

The day of my dissertation defense came with a queasy sensation at the pit of my stomach. I dressed up in my best black pants suit from my job market misadventures. I left my Main Street apartment to the campus. As I drove over the Chenango River Bridge, feeling bizarre, I thought:

"This is my last morning driving to Binghamton University as a graduate student." It was surreal.

I thought a lot of persons would be at my dissertation defense - like the daunting crowd at the defense of my prospectus. But it wasn't so. There were only one of my fellow Jamaicans there, along with the members of my dissertation committee. I went through the presentation of my three papers, answered questions from my committee and that was it. I had become Dr. Sophia C. Terrelonge. They all congratulated me with my new title. The whole thing felt anti-climactic. After all my sleepless nights and extreme angst through the years of grad school, this is it? While I was happy that my degree was complete, I felt sad inside. The fact that I didn't have a job made everything feel more dismal.

I met with my dissertation supervisor a few times to resolve the final details of my papers. I then started the arduous task of fitting all my papers into the dissertation format given by the Graduate School. It was a long, annoying process. I had to create section breaks, pay close attention the font size, line spacing and paragraph spacing.

I was convinced that someone in the Graduate School was out to get me. My electronic submissions kept coming back with things to be fixed. I finally had it when it came back the last time from the same annoying female in that office.

I didn't know her and I had never spoken to her before. I kid you not: I got into a holy anger! I did real spiritual warfare on her case. I sent in my dissertation again. It was accepted. Hallelujah! Finally, I was done with this Ph.D.! I felt like I could breathe again. Whew! Hallelujah! Glory to God! ☺

Afterthoughts

In retrospect, this moment of completing my education was a great occasion. I was facing the uncertainty of unexpected unemployment, but I still had a glimmer of hope. During this period and the ones to come, I had many such small blessings. However, I can only see them now. At the time of my trials, I could not recognize them because I was so focused on what was lacking.

Beloved, it is certain that we will undergo challenges in this life. I encourage you to never live life as though it consists of large chunks of great moments. Recognize that we operate in a continuum of seasons, which contain wonderful, bad and neutral moments. Celebrate the small blessings in your life, especially the ones that come in the middle of your storms. Life is not perfect, but it is made up of perfect moments. Remember Luke 16:10:

> *"He who is faithful in what is least, is faithful also in much;*

and he who is unjust in what is least, is unjust also in much."

Please be grateful to Jesus for your small blessings. Hold on in faith and be encouraged. Your bigger blessings will manifest in His divine timing.

Chapter 6
Graduation... What's Next?

Graduation was bitter-sweet. It was wonderful that I was finished. I felt victorious! But the bitterness seeped into my joy. I had no job, and a job was my security blanket. A job meant money. Money meant a safe place to rest my head, a way to pay the bills, and a means to keep me fed, clothed and healthy. At the time, money was everything to me. I was transfixed by my impending lack of finances which would hit right after my last SUNY Binghamton check.

I became more depressed, remembering that my mother died right before I began my doctoral journey. Mommy would never see me in my graduation gown and cap, walking across that stage to accept my final degree. I would not even have the consolation prize of any relatives coming to my graduation. Those relatives (who would have desired to be there) did not have a US visa.

I was determined to go through the graduation ceremony despite my deep sadness and my impending financial crisis. At my Bachelor of Science graduation at UWI Mona, Mommy was there, along with my elder sister, her husband and their children, my nieces. I didn't bother attending my Master of Science graduation ceremony, as we were beginning to worry about my mother's breast lumps. Back then I worked at UWI, so I just never celebrated my second degree. I had embarked on my doctoral studies immediately after my mother's burial. I still wanted to attend my final graduation and have a good time (however fleeting) and cheer myself on.

My finances were stretched. I could pay for my gown and hat, but my budget could not accommodate a new outfit. I paid homage to my mother by wearing a thigh-length, earth-toned jacket from one of her dresses, along with a black top and a pair of black slacks. My dissertation supervisor had given me a graduation gift of a silver chain with an intricate cross pendant. It served to complete my graduation ceremony attire. I arranged my shoulder-length dreadlocks, put on face powder and lip gloss, and doused myself in my favorite perfume. I was making payments on a used silver Hyundai Santa Fe for the past year or so. I got in my Santa Fe and drove myself, all alone, to my graduation.

Other graduates were rushing about to join the procession into the venue. I saw all my professors, received congratulations and I also congratulated my fellow graduates. We were all happy and eager to start the ceremony. I felt like I was floating on air as I marched in time to the processional music and into the grand, light-filled space. I got to the end! Ms. Adlin wash-belly[19] was now a Doctor! Hallelujah!

I got to my seat and observed all the protocols of the event. We went through all the speeches and responses. Then we finally got to my long-awaited moment: being hooded and accepting my doctoral degree! I felt my heart jump into my throat when I joined the line to await my turn on the stage. I was a happy nervous wreck! Finally, I heard my name. I climbed the stage and stood before my dissertation supervisor to be hooded. I flashed a double thumbs-up to the camera and that photo became one of the highlights for the 2015 SUNY Binghamton graduation ceremony. I collected my doctoral degree, took the final set of photos and returned to my seat.

The graduation ceremony ended. I saw graduates surrounded by living and loving relatives and friends, taking photos, smiling, laughing, hugging...and I felt all alone again. No one was there for me. I proceeded outside the venue and the same scenes repeated themselves. I even took photos of three other celebratory family unions,

---

19 "Wash-belly" refers to the last child born to a woman.

while smiling and hiding my own unhappiness.

The Graduate School reception was convivial and the food was good. We were so stuffed that we (new graduates and existing grad students) scratched our prior plan to go to a nearby Chinese restaurant. The reception soon ended and everyone dispersed to their own celebrations. I went back to my same apartment, all alone. As the door clicked shut, the gloom took over. How long would I be able to stay in that apartment?

I turned the lights on and got a drink of water from the kitchen. I sat down at my table in the living room and looked around. I heaved a heavy sigh and I worried again about my survival. The clouds in my mind were heavy with foreboding. The little light left in me was running away. My world got steadily darker. I began my downward spiral into depression.

Afterthoughts

It's amazing how we can fixate on the things that go wrong around us. We just can't seem to release the negative in our situations. Beloved, it's very important that we learn to control our minds, because that's where our reality originates.[20] We need to remember that life is not perfect, but it consists of perfect moments. Let us always celebrate

---

20 Proverbs 4:23.

these perfect moments, no matter how small they are, or the context in which they occur. Let us rejoice always in the Lord.[21]

Money is not everything. We have heard this saying many times. But why do some of us still think and act as if it is everything? Some of us live our lives in pursuit of more promotions, to get more money, to buy more stuff. I'm not advocating that we all adopt minimalism, but at what point do we recognize and reject this fixation? Is money useful? Yes. Is money intrinsically evil? No. So what's the matter then? The problem arises when we are in love with it, when we are obsessed with it. This makes money an idol in our hearts. Idolatry is a sin, as we cannot truly love and serve Jesus Christ and still cling to this obsession. It's either Jesus alone, or Jesus none at all.[22]

I am not perfect in this regard. As I stated before, I was obsessed with money. I saw it as security, my safety net from the poverty that I experienced in my childhood. I kept getting prompts from the Holy Spirit about this issue, but I would not pay much attention to Him. The events that I experienced were all divinely planned. They made me realize that money, mammon, is not my security. Jesus Christ is my only source of security. We should always obey

---

21 Philippians 4:10-13, 1 Thessalonians 5: 16-18 and Philippians 4:4.
22 1 Timothy 6:10, Matthew 6:24; Exodus 34:14, Exodus 20:1-6, Deuteronomy 4:24, and Hebrews 12:29.

the prompts of the Holy Spirit and be quick to repent. Let us truly walk by faith and not by sight.[23] Know that even when we can't see it, Jesus has everything secured.

---

23 2 Corinthians 5:7.

Chapter 7

Relocation: Moving on Downwards?

I had my last hurrah when I graduated. I had nothing else to move on to: no tenure-track academic position, no industry position, nothing. I was in a foreign land with no close relatives. Whatever friends I had, they were busy enjoying their lives. I was single and feeling quite aged at 31. Marriage had not happened. The 2.5 children and the white picket fence also had not happened. I had dedicated over three decades of my life to my education. What drove this single-minded quest? I was determined not to live the life that my mother had suffered.

I sunk deeper into depression for every week that passed and I was still unemployed. I felt broken and forgotten by God. I was attending the same church and I was doing my fasting and prayers like clock-work. I wasn't praying for any husband. All I wanted was a job in the USA. I had many days of seclusion and fasting sessions. My savings dwindled all through the summer of 2015.

My apartment's living room window overlooked a bus stop, the apartment's parking space and my car. Right across the adjacent Schubert Avenue was Dunkin Donuts, which saw me frequently. I "sugar highed" my way through spells of depression. I could walk about 10 minutes to a grocery store located within a small plaza. I was 5 minutes away via car from downtown Binghamton. It was a great place to live.

By the end of July 2015, I had exhausted my finances that were saved from my graduate assistantship. I was now down to a US$50 per week food bill (if the electric bill came through, my food bill would be halved). I lost weight and I developed a bald spot in the middle of my head from the stress. My bra-strap-length dreadlocks began to weaken and break off close to my scalp. I had my hair tied in scarves all the time, because my head resembled a forest ravaged by woodcutters removing trees in random places.

I couldn't keep the Main Street apartment. I respected my landlords too much to keep living in their space knowing that I couldn't afford it. Earlier in the summer, I had asked their secretary to change my rent collection schedule by a few days. Now I was at the wall. There was no alternative but to move out.

I desperately looked for a cheaper apartment in Binghamton, but soon discovered that my landlords were very kind. I was living in an underpriced apartment, as studios were now the same price as my one-bedroom. I expanded my search to the neighboring city of Endicott, but it was the same story. Finally I followed the Union Center Main Highway, to a motel. They had tiny studios with a bed, dresser, a table, two chairs and a mini fridge atop a second dresser. This option allowed me to pay US$115 per week inclusive of all utilities except internet. This place was dingy and run-down. The other occupants were all very poor white folks. Unfortunately, the majority of these persons were either addicts or recovering addicts. They spent their days smoking on the sparse porch areas. It was a hopeless atmosphere. It represented a reality that very few Jamaicans would believe exist in the "heaven" that America was thought to be.

On July 30, 2015, U-Haul sent me two assistants (a man and a woman) to help me pack my furniture into a U-box. They complained bitterly about having to move my sleeper sofa down one flight of stairs and tried to get me to book a second U-box. I knew that was not in my budget. I showed them how to pack that U-box like only a Jamaican could! They drove the U-box off to their storage facility in downtown Binghamton, marveling that they were able to close the door at all!

I slept on an air mattress on my living room floor, surrounded by my remaining bags that would go into my car in the morning. Depression pressed me down into that beautiful hardwood floor. The next day, I got up early, ate what was left in the fridge and packed most of the bags into my car. I cleaned the apartment very well and checked all the cupboards and nooks for any stray belongings. I then took my final shower and slowly dressed. I lingered a bit, gazing around the empty space that was once full of hope and life. I thought about that dark, musty, tiny studio that I would inhabit in a few hours. I was depressed, but resolute. I could no longer afford that light-filled, airy, centrally-located apartment, so I had to go.

I stepped out and locked the door on my life at Main Street, Binghamton. I hurried down, saying goodbye to a fellow tenant, and fled into my car. I was too downtrodden to even cry. I was an empty shell and in auto-pilot mode; nothing mattered and I cared very little. I drove downtown to the landlords' office and handed over the keys that were no longer mine to keep. They said that I was a great tenant, and should I need a reference, to give them a call. They also wished me good luck in my endeavors and then I left.

I stopped at the Vestal Walmart to buy a zipped mattress cover. There was no way that I would put my sheets on a mattress that so many random folks slept on! I drove out to the boondocks that would now become my home. I stopped at the last supermarket along that dreary highway to nowhere. I picked up some cheap sausages, canned vegs, rice and bread that would serve for dinner and breakfast.

I pulled into the potholed lot of the dingy motel. There were few persons present to witness my moving in. I went to pay for my first two weeks, which then became my payment routine. I struggled with my bags up to that second-floor corner room. The room's only saving grace was a large picture window looking onto a leafy green tree and the T-junction. That window was my joy in the summer and fall, as I watched cars go by with camping gear and beautiful RVs going on vacation. I enviously watched the rich drive past with their yachts, cruising off to enjoy the surrounding lakes. The same window also became a pain in winter when it let through a cold draft. It was an alternate universe that was the polar opposite of all my great expectations.

More darkness entered my life, slowly draining me of the will to survive. It seemed that Jesus had gone deaf and wasn't paying much attention to me. I began to wonder what I had done to Him. Why He would punish me with unemployment? Nothing made sense. I felt like He was pranking me, and it was not at all funny! In my mind, Jesus had started towards the exit door.

Afterthoughts

My tendency to "awful-ize" adverse events didn't help at all. At the time, I didn't even want to exist anymore. Beloved, you will experience bad situations, really bad ones. It's easier said than done, but: Don't freak out! If you freak out, it will neither change the situation, nor will it make you feel better inside. I wish that I had the faith, then, to believe that Jesus would ultimately work all things out for my good.[24]

Do not let your present adverse circumstances trick you into believing that your entire life will be a long symphony of sorrow, pain and woe. No set of circumstances are permanent. The hard times teach us valuable lessons, and they make us resilient. Most importantly, they push us closer to Christ. There is no child of Christ who has triumphed over an intense struggle, who has not had a deeper knowledge and appreciation of Him. That person also received greater anointing and grew more in the characteristics of Jesus Christ.[25]

Beloved, let Jesus Christ be the only one to define your life - not your job (or lack thereof), not your money (or

---

24 Romans 8:28.
25 Please read and meditate on Romans 8:35-39, 1 John 5:4-5, John 16:33, 1 Peter 1:3-9 and James 1:3-4.

lack thereof), not your social ranking, not your peers, not your parents, not your spouses, not your family. As born-again Christians, we are "a chosen generation" and "a royal priesthood".[26] The only thing that matters is how our King and High Priest, Jesus Christ sees us! Our definition is in Jesus Christ: nothing and no one else. He is the Great Potter, who uses all of our past experiences to mold us into vessels fit for His glorious work on earth.[27] Let us all follow Jesus Christ and focus on Him alone as the center of our lives.

---

26 1 Peter 2:9-10.
27 2 Timothy 2:20-21.

Chapter 8

The Famine

I woke up disoriented in a dingy studio apartment with sounds of the neighbors calling out to each other. I had left the window cracked open overnight to let the heat escape from the room. The window now let in the foul-smelling aroma of cheap cigarettes. A man who lived downstairs also enjoyed the view of the T-junction just outside my window. He would have his morning smoke every day (except in winter) right under my window. Every morning I would shut my window until he left me to enjoy the fresh air again.

That room had an old mustard green carpet that I could never get completely clean. I discovered that a nice family of mold had moved into the closet. This was due to the damp that spread along the outside wall of the building. No matter how much I cleaned those areas with bleach and soap, the mold just grew back.

The studio was uncomfortable. In the last days of summer, I was hot and miserable. In the fall months, it was bearable. In the winter, I was frozen. I bundled up in layers of clothes and a blanket, but I was still freezing. I could not believe how difficult my life had become, in spite of my dedication to following Jesus.

I now lived very far from the church that I attended in Binghamton, and gas was expensive. I noticed a local church along the highway, which I decided to visit. The church was filled with mainly white parishioners. They were friendly, and so I began attending church there. I told them that I was job hunting and living off my savings. What I didn't tell them was that those savings were from back home in Jamaica. I also didn't tell them that the savings were rapidly dwindling due to the stronger US exchange rate and the bank transfer fees. I was destitute. However, since I had my car and my nice clothes (bought in better times), I didn't look like I was suffering. I didn't trust anyone, so I continued to suffer in silence and sunk deeper into depression.

I began to do my fasting and prayer sessions again. My three days, five days and even one week fasting sessions were imbued with my desperation and fatigue from life. I did these multi-day fasts two, and sometimes three times per month. I wouldn't eat during daylight hours. I would only read my Bible, pray, listen to gospel music and sometimes sleep. I would only eat in the evening.

It was a repetitive meal of canned baked beans cooked with chopped sausages, and served with white rice. I cooked all my meals atop a two-burner countertop stove, accompanied by cold water from my mini fridge.

My days of fasting were fortuitous, not only for my soul's sake, but for my wallet. By eating once per day, for sometimes two to three weeks, I was able to make my food stretch. It was a blessing in disguise that I only had the US$115 weekly rent to pay (which also covered my electricity, water and heat). I had to buy drinking water, as the water quality was bad. I only used the tap water for external purposes when a lot of soap and disinfectants were also in play.

I watched my savings deplete as I continued to wait for a job to turn up. I received my Optional Practical Training (OPT) work card back in July 2015 before I left Binghamton. The card was a continuation of my F-1 (or student) visa. It was designed to allow US-degreed foreigners the chance to transition to H1-B status.[28]

I had decided against any kind of visa fraud by doing a "business" marriage. I believe that marriage should be reserved for the godly and genuine love between the man

---

28 The H1-B visa allows foreigners who were trained in the USA to also work in the USA. However this visa is only issued if a foreigner is employed by a US-based firm who completes the paperwork (or does the sponsorship) for that visa.

and woman concerned. I was not going to do any such marital union just to remain in the USA. I was determined to do things the legal and the right way. This decision cost me one long-term friendship/mentorship, as the person thought that I was mad to refuse a "business" marriage. The person said I was "unwise" to wait on a US employer to sponsor me a H1-B visa. But I was resolute.

I kept applying for jobs. Going to Barnes and Noble for their internet was no longer feasible due to the gas cost. So I got my internet installed, which meant that I could apply for jobs all the time. I applied for jobs that required a Ph.D., a Masters, a first degree and even high school certificates. I was in a state of complete desperation that no one in Jamaica was aware of. I desperately needed to work in order to survive. Despite my best efforts, I was broke. I was down to my last US$500 in savings. I was like the widow in Zarephath to whom God sent the Prophet Elijah.[29] I was preparing for my last. If God didn't come through with some sort of employment, then I really didn't know what would happen.

---

29 This biblical story is recorded in 1 Kings 17:7-16.

Afterthoughts

Being "good"[30] and trying to faithfully follow Jesus does not mean an easy life. Unfortunately, bad things happen to "good" people. The examples of Paul, Peter, James, Andrew and the other early apostles support this stance. They were all devout followers of Jesus Christ who endured gruesome beatings and imprisonment for the Gospel. Some of them were also martyred. They were obedient unto death.[31] Now how does that history put our problems into perspective? I find that my problems pale in comparison to the suffering of the early church. At this time, most of us are free to worship Jesus Christ without such hazards. But, some of our brethren are not so fortunate and we should pray for them and assist in any way that we can.

I was so worried about what other people would think about the state of my life. Maybe I could have gotten help during that season. But I was unwilling to unveil myself and my situation. I wanted to remain hidden. While I remained hidden, the enemy had a field day keeping me in constant depression. Beloved, pride often keeps us from reaching out for the help that we need. Pride is present

---

30 Here are some reminders about our self-righteousness: Proverbs 16:2, 2 Corinthians 10:18, Isaiah 64:6 and 1 John 1:8-10.
31 Please refer to Hebrews 12:3-4. For good measure, you should read the entire chapter, as well as Hebrews 11.

in all of us and it is a sin.[32] Lord, purge us from the sin of pride! When we pretend that all is well and it is not so, we give the devil permission to afflict us.[33] When we are willing to reveal what's happening with us, we receive deliverance in Christ Jesus.

> *Lord Jesus, I pray for your beloved children who are going through turbulent times. Almighty God, release them from the yoke of pride and every other chain by the power in Your Name and in Your Blood Lord Jesus! Please lead them to your appointed persons and organizations to get the support they need. Father, surround them with Your love and mercy right now. I declare that it is well with each of them in Jesus' name. Amen.*

---

32 Please see 1 John 2:15-17.
33 Please read James 5:13-16 and Matthew 18:18-20.

Chapter 9

Survival by any (Legal) Means Necessary

I was down to US$300 in October 2015. I could only pay for an extra two weeks rent and some food. I looked up to Jesus and wondered where He was. I got no positive answers from my applications. The full-time jobs were looking for persons who already had US permanent residence (or a green card). Most companies that I interviewed with were clueless about how to apply for the H1-B visa. Once I told them I would need that authorization before my OPT permit expired in a year, it was game over!

Survival now had me applying for jobs that would not keep me on long-term, but would at least allow me to live. I contacted an Endicott call center that was hiring for customer service representatives (CSRs). The lady on the line asked if I could come in to see them that day. I was happy! I went to the brief interview, signed some documents to authorize my background check, and did a mouth-swab drug test. All of this happened on the Tuesday. On the Friday of that same week, I was back in their offices completing the necessary paperwork, and got invited for a two-week paid training the following Monday, which was now November 2015. Hallelujah!

Customer service training was interesting because it was new to me. I made sure that no one knew (except for the administrators) that I had a Ph.D. I told everyone that I came from Jamaica to study for a degree in Economics. Everyone just assumed that it was my first degree and I didn't bother to correct their mistake. I was already emotionally battered. I didn't need my new workplace to become another avenue to lower my self-esteem.

Training was repetitive and the trainer only read from the PowerPoint slides and documents. The morning of the day that we were to go live,[34] we had an in-class demonstration. One person played a difficult customer while the other played the CSR. We practiced how to answer a call, what key words to use to calm down a customer, etc. This exercise was very useful, but it was only done the day that we would go live!

Then I had to go live. I sat down gingerly at my assigned desk. All the other seasoned CSRs mockingly looked on.

34 "Going live" means going on the actual call center floor to field calls from real customers.

I couldn't understand their cynicism, but I soon figured it out. There were two computer screens, one was for the internal call log process; the other was for the client's[35] websites. The telephone had an integrated switchboard to answer calls, put calls on hold and have up to three active calls at a time. I was nervous, but soon settled into a rhythm at the end of the day. I went home tired, but relieved.

I worked Mondays to Fridays from 8:00 AM to 5:00 PM. The building was a cold industrial concrete façade with a few glazed glass surfaces. We were paid every fortnight at US$9 per hour. It was a dreary job. The call center floor was so frigid that even my jacket could not help. And the tiny cubicles were packed tight, so one person's flu, soon became everyone's flu. There were no sick days: if you slipped, you would slide out of that job.

I kept my lunch in my backpack, which I stowed under my desk on the production floor. We could keep our personal belongings with us on the call floor, as we were watched by both multiple security cameras and section supervisors. We could not go into our bags while on the floor, and all our cell phones needed to be on silent. We went to lunch as per the instructions of the section supervisors.

---

35 A call center offers CSR services to businesses or "clients". Therefore one call center would field calls from several companies' customers.

Everyone soon knew me as the girl with a boring palate (that's what I told the nosy ones anyways). I was always eating some mac-and-cheese with pieces of meat inside. Other times, it would be Jamaican-style rice-and-peas, with said pieces of meat included. Every day, I would heat my little food container in one of the lunchroom's microwaves.

I was determined to save, as I had no idea how long this job would last. Every payday would see these CSRs (some with multiple children) ordering relatively expensive Chinese lunches or pizzas for delivery. My mouth would water as I watched them eat their delicious food. But I kept focused and pretended like my mac-and-cheese (or rice-and-peas) concoctions were the greatest thing ever! I had gone through my famine season. I was determined not to waste any further resources for the rest of my life.

Soon fatigue began to set in. I was working my US$9 per hour job with random rude customers cursing me out. I especially remember one lady who called in. As a part of our role, we always had to go through a verification process by asking customers their names and other account details. I began the name verification part. Her name started with a "D" but I was hearing something else. So I said: "D as in dog?"

Now why did I say that? She went off on me straight away!

"What dog? Are you calling me a dog? *Your mother is a dog!* Why can't you people use anything else other than "D as in dog?""

She also rained down expletives on me. Now you can curse out a Jamaican all you want, but do not say anything about our mothers! Take my advice, never "diss"[36] a Jamaican's mother - we do not take kindly to such.

I went silent on my end of the phone. I thought to myself: If I didn't need this stupid call center job and if I wasn't a professing Christian, I would have answered her very well! But I held my peace.[37]

She went on cursing and carrying on, burning up her phone credit while I remained silent. Finally, she said: "Hello? Are you there?"

After about two heart beats I replied: "Yes I'm still here. Let's try this again: D as in donuts?"

She responded: "Yes, that's better!"

I had so many disgusting calls that I began to believe the classic stereotype of the rude American. I was sick and tired of the whole call center hierarchy of disrespect and disregard for the CSRs. I was tired of the in-fighting

---

36 The term "diss" in the Jamaican vernacular means "disrespect".
37 Ephesians 4:29-32.

and politics on the call floor, as people jostled to have the highest call rate.[38] I was tired of feeling like I was in high school again, with the "mean girls" group activated times ten. I just came to have such a deep revulsion for that place.

There was also a spiritual dimension where the energy was so demonic. We had a variety of persons who were into the occult. There were also a myriad of calls coming into that one space. I had a revelation of shadows hovering over the call floor and converging around the center concrete column in the middle of that room. Every time I passed that column, my head would feel heavy. I was praying in tongues so much on that job it wasn't funny! When I slept, I had dreams of answering calls. I also had nightmares of not being able to assist customers who desperately needed my help. This was much to the disapproval and disparage of my supervisors. On weekends I couldn't even relax. I dreaded going back to work from Friday night, all the way through to Sunday night. I was traumatized.

I became a machine, devoid of feeling. Alarm. Get up. Prayer and scripture. Eat breakfast. Pack lunch. Shower. Get dressed. Leave home. Drive to work through traffic. Clock in. Survive the day. Clock out. Drive

---

38 My best average call rate was 8 calls per hour, while others were doing an average of 15 calls per hour!

home. Eat dinner. Prepare for bed. Rinse and repeat.

I was nothing. All my degrees meant nothing; they were totally useless in my eyes. I would angrily ask God why He allowed me to get all of these degrees. What was the point if He wasn't going to provide commensurate employment, salary and benefits? All those hours of studying, doing exams and writing papers were just for a US$9 per hour job! I began to doubt that Jesus was even present in my life. I was exhausted and burnt out. I was a shell of a human being with nothing inside.

Afterthoughts

Sometimes life just hammers us down into the ground. At times, the jobs that we do in order to survive actually drain us of the will to live, to feel, to be...human. Toxic supervisors, co-workers and working conditions, can all wreak havoc on our bodies, souls, minds and spirits. I get it! It's very hard! But, we have to be grateful for the small blessings, just as much as we are grateful for the grand ones. Never despise small beginnings. The greatest trees that tower over the forest floor all had their beginnings in the smallest seeds, hidden in the ground.

As you are in the middle of your growing season, do not fall into the comparison trap. When we compare our lives and possessions to others, we only put extra burden on ourselves. We will never be like anyone else. I can only be me, and you can only be you. Stop coveting what other people have! You have a unique God-created blueprint for your life. And guess what? Your blueprint calls for certain bespoke processes that no one else has to go through!

Love yourself, be grateful for what you have and grow in accordance with Jesus' plan for your life. No situation is permanent. Be encouraged. You are growing daily in Christ, and you are a masterpiece in the making. It may not look like it right now, but trust Jesus. When the tapestry of your life is finally revealed, it will be breathtakingly beautiful! ☺

Chapter 10

Lord, Haven't I Suffered Enough?

I spent a horrible winter freezing in bed every night due to the draughty large window that wouldn't completely close. It got so bad that ice formed on the inside of that window - right over my bed! The mold in the closet spread even more.

The air in my tiny studio was a mix of anxiety, sickness, poverty, coldness and mustiness. I suffered from bad head colds, and my job insurance could barely pay for doctor's visits. And so I dosed myself every day with over-the-counter (OTC) cold medicines. I was depressed and sick throughout that winter. Even when the bone-deep cold would fail to sneak under my multi-layered bed coverings, I had no peace. I would have the familiar nightmares of the call floor. Although I was working, I didn't alter my menu much from when I was unemployed. I saved assiduously to ward off the possibility of yet another famine.

Every weekday, my suffering started at 6:45 AM in the harsh winter air. My breath would freeze, as I struggled to free my car's tires from the snowfall. The ice would malignantly cling to all my mirrors. It defied all my attempts to use the can of defroster to de-ice my car. As the winter went on, I began to go outside at 6:30 AM to get enough lead time to fight the ice monster. Above all, I had to make my 8:00 AM log-in at work.

I would often get inside my car and realize that my frost-bitten fingers couldn't grip the steering wheel. The good winter gloves were expensive, and doubling up my old winter ones never worked. I would sit in the still cold car, crying in pain as my fingers fought themselves back to life. I wondered each time why I had to suffer like this. My Ph.D. was completely useless. I felt gutted.

Winter trapped me inside that cold industrial space during breaks and lunch times. So, I endured the snarky colleagues and spoke very little about my personal life. I needed this job to survive. But I felt like I surrendered a little piece of my soul every time I swiped into that grey building. I was low in my body, soul, mind and spirit. I was stripped of all my humanity. I felt as cold and barren as the winter I saw outside every day.

I continued to attend the local church. I worshipped and smiled with them for the few hours, but I didn't let them in. I could not abide the possibility of denigration and the label of laziness if I complained about this job. I felt being that vulnerable would make me play into any stereotypes they may hold about my race and my "foreignness".

I continued my job applications every weekend. The call center snatched so much of my will, that I couldn't do anything worthwhile once I got home each evening. I continued to be an automaton. I was Sophia Terrelonge, Machine Number _____.[39] I was not human.

I kept getting rejections from my applications, even though they were non-academic vacancies. I couldn't afford to participate in yet another academic job market search due to my work schedule and finances. But there was a part of me that was still hopeful.

Soon winter began to morph into the promise of spring. The ice was no longer so tenacious, and I began to have brighter mornings and brighter evenings. However, the dark clouds began to gather at work. The project/client that I worked for, was a major natural gas company in the mid-west. The spring meant gas usage would begin to decline. We processed fewer connections and more disconnections. The management team began whispering among themselves. They eyed us more frequently, some with looks of pity, and others with malignant delight. We

---

39 I don't remember the ID number I had at this job.

knew that the lay-offs would begin.

We began to notice that there was a lot of "pulling" of persons (mid-shift) off the call floor and into meetings with management. Then one member of the management team would come onto the call floor to collect that worker's personal belongings and take them away. We would never see that person again. We all knew that our time would come soon. Colleagues who worked the more stable projects/clients looked on with whatever pity they could muster up from their jaded selves.

One Monday evening, I got a call for a Skype interview the next day. I wrestled with my choice of work versus interview. Eventually I decided that the call center would soon fire me anyways, so it would be best to go for the job interview. I called in late that Tuesday morning. My supervisor's tone made me know that I would be terminated that day. I gave the interview my best, but... I did not get the job.

I got in late to the call center. I was strangely calm and smiling that Tuesday. I felt very much at peace. When I walked in and sat down at my station, one woman gave me the evil eye - the call volume was heavy that day. But I was unmoved and still calm. I logged into one of the systems, when predictably I was pulled off the floor for a meeting with management. I smiled, which freaked out my supervisor. I calmly packed my scarf and jacket into my backpack. I wanted everything to be easy for them to pick up and take to me outside. I then logged out of everything, got up and walked smiling to that meeting. The persons who weren't busy on calls, whispered among themselves.

Of course, they pulled random recordings of my calls and made their accusations about protocols that were not followed. They told me that I could no longer work there. I was unfazed. I sat there smiling. They asked me if I had anything to say. I said I didn't and asked if that would be all. I returned their ID card. I settled when to expect my last pay check. I then thanked them all and left the room. Another supervisor went back to get my backpack - we all knew the drill. I thanked her and left, smiling all the way to my car.

Once I got outside, I lifted my hands in the cool spring air and shouted: "I'm free! Hallelujah!" I burst into a giddy fit of laughter. A supervisor followed me into the parking lot: they probably thought that I was planning to damage their cars. But she was disappointed. I beeped my horn at her as I sped out of that parking lot to my freedom. I can honestly say that the call center is the worst place that I have ever worked. I welcomed being fired from that job!

My rehabilitation from the call center would take a month. During that period, I continued to have the usual nightmares. I got to tutor online for a Christian university in March 2016 and they paid me every fortnight. However, it was far less than the previous job paid, so I began to freak out. How would I survive? I had saved up about US$3500 from the call center, but I knew that it would soon run out even with my frugality.

I could find no other part-time job. They would lose interest as soon as they heard that my work permit would expire in July 2016. I was in a quandary. All I could think was: "When would God stop hating me? What did I do to You Jesus? Please tell me so that I can repent quickly. Stop punishing me Jesus! I just can't take it anymore! Please Jesus, just stop!"

Afterthoughts

There are times when we go through fiery circumstances, which destroy everything that we know and possess. It's as if we did some grievous sin and we are now being chastised. It feels like we are being punished. But this is not always true. Before the Potter can mold us, He has to break us. Breaking is never easy, it is never pleasant. However, it is a necessary process for us to become vessels of honor unto Him.[40]

---

40 Jeremiah 18:1-4 and 2 Timothy 2:20-21.

During this period of turmoil, I could no longer write creatively. My creative energy and mental acuity were at zero level. However the Lord led me to write scriptures and messages that I would hear from Him at the back of my Bible. The Holy Spirit led me to go back to this specific Bible to read what I wrote that month after my termination. In April 2016, there were two messages:

April 3, 2016
Luke 24:21

You may think that all is gone, dead and lost. But I AM the God of revival and resurrection. There is nothing too hard for me to do.

April 26, 2016
Ezekiel 37:1-10

The Lord will cause all dry bones to spring to life once more. He will cause the breath of life to enter all areas of your existence. He will do this to show you and everyone around you that He is GOD, THE LORD GOD ALMIGHTY.

Hallelujah! It is not over for you! We serve a God who specializes in resurrecting dead things. Stand firmly in the belief that whatever seems dead for you and within you, whatever the people around you are saying is dead, God can and He will resurrect! They are getting ready for funeral rites, but God is saying: "Not yet! Part 2 is coming!" Beloved, you will not die, but live![41] You will live to declare the glorious work of Jesus Christ in the land of the living! Believe in Him and wait for your resurrection hour! Glory to God!

41 Psalm 118:17.

Chapter 11

Praying and Fasting Like a Mad Woman!

I felt that Jesus had rejected me because I did something bad. I spent sleepless nights trying to remember if I had any sins for which I didn't repent. I even "re-repented" of anything that I deemed could make Jesus not like me and deliver His judgment upon me. I resumed my marathon fasts - three days, five days and seven days. I was back to eating once a day. I became more psychotic as the days went by. I tried to win back God's love and to get back into His good books. I wanted to become His favorite who He loved and blessed.

I truly believe that I became borderline psychotic. I would shut myself up in my tiny studio, fasting and praying and speaking in tongues. Some of my drug-crazed neighbors began to think that I was the crazy one. Every time I went outside to the mailbox, to dump my garbage or to go to the grocery store, the air was unfriendly. I was accosted by their furtive glances of discomfort and aborted whispers. I didn't care; I just needed to get back into right standing with God.

The Jamaican gospel music and Hillsong lyric videos could no longer calm me. I looked further back to the motherland, to the African continent, to Nigeria in particular. I went back for songs birthed from suffering and pain with a hopeful outlook and eventual deliverance. I started with Sinach and made my way through much of the Believers Love World gospel artistes. I then explored other Nigerian and West African gospel musicians. I even began singing in the Igbo and Yoruba languages, although I didn't fully understand what I sang. However, I was somewhat soothed - like how a child with no language skills is soothed by her mother's voice. My anthems became Preye Odede's *Ebezina* (to which I would weep bitterly despite being told in the song not to do so), Monique's *Power Flow* and Sinach's *Way Maker* and *I Know Who I Am*.

The marathon day fasts became marathon night vigils. Soon my neighbors stopped whispering and glared at me angrily. I was disturbing their sleep, but my insomnia, depression and my fight to not become suicidal, would not let me give them any peace. I saw them as demon-possessed. I thought that they didn't want to hear about

Jesus, as they were trying to stifle my praise. I couldn't see their side of things - incomprehensible words and noises from a foreigner. But, I can now see their perspective.

The neighbors made many complaints to the resident manager, even to the owners of the building. Both manager and landlord spoke to me about disturbing the nightly peace. They informed me that I would need to leave if I couldn't keep quiet. Events escalated until one evening at about 7:00 PM, I heard a pounding on my studio door while I was in the shower.

"Who is it?" I called from the shower.

"Police! Open up!" said a strong male voice.

What kind of police is this now? I had never had the law called on me before! These people are the devil incarnate!

"I'm in the shower! Give me a minute to get out!" I called back.

I got out of the shower, soap still all over me and hurriedly dressed up. I got to the door and opened it to a white young man, in police garb, with a book in his hand.

He said: "We've had a report of loud noises and thudding coming from your apartment from the neighbors downstairs."

I went immediately into wisdom mode: "Thudding? I don't understand, I was only opening and closing my cupboards to get dinner ready. I just finished eating and was getting my shower to rest for the evening when you knocked."

Anyways, the officer took my full name, driver's license number and telephone number. He cautioned me to be a little bit more careful especially in the evening hours. Then he left in his squad car, with its multi-colored roof lights blinking in the darkness. I believe that he realized that the call was a vengeful one.

Of course, you know that I still prayed and listened to my gospel music - I just didn't sing along with the songs at nights. And of course, I did pray against those persons downstairs who called the police on me to arrest me - when I wasn't even doing anything at the time! I didn't know their names, but they were the subject of many night prayers. Eventually the woman immediately below me moved out. Then the man in the next room beside her lost his job and became fixed in his room just like me.

I started to climb down from my mania - I was still troubled in my spirit, but at least I was under some control. I began to remind God of all the things that I thought were signs that He would provide legal long-term employment for me in the USA. The Spirit of God continued to give me scriptures and encouragement that I would record in the back of my Bible. I encouraged myself, and I became more stable mentally, emotionally and spiritually. However I was still hopeful that some job would come through with the H1-B visa before my work permit and the subsequent 60-day grace period expired. I exercised my last bit of faith in this matter.

Afterthoughts

Jesus was not punishing me; I was simply undergoing my breaking process. The breaking was necessary to mold me into His dedicated vessel. Jesus loves me unconditionally. There is nothing I can do (or not do) to win His unending love. It is freely given. I want you to know that you are truly loved. Jesus loves you unconditionally. You cannot bargain for, and you cannot lose His love.[42]

My birthday is May 12th, and back then, I was not looking forward to my birthday. Let me share that month's Bible entries with you:

May 11, 2016
2:30 PM
John 14:23-27 and John 15:1-16

"I love you, I AM with you. Abide in Me Sophia, abide in Me." <u>Jesus</u>

---

42 John 3:16-17, John 10:17-18 and 2 Corinthians 5:14-21.

May 12, 2016
Mark 11:22-26

Be steadfast in your faith in Christ. Believe that He will grant you your earnest request in due season.

May 25, 2016
3:30 AM
1 Kings 18:41-46

"I will pour out my rain, my abundant rain on your dry places. Be patient and wait earnestly, because I will bring the abundance of rain upon you." <u>GOD</u>

Beloved, you are the apple of Jesus' eye[43] and He knows everything about you.[44] He does care.[45] He loves you tirelessly and He will love you forever.[46] He's got you and He's got your situation. Know that Jesus Christ will work all things for your good and to His glory.[47] Know that you are deeply and eternally loved.

---

43 Zechariah 2:8. It would be good if you read the entire chapter for context.
44 Isaiah 44:24-28 and Psalm 139:13-18.
45 1 Peter 5:7, Psalm 55:22 and Psalm 56:3-4.
46 1 Chronicles 16:34, 1 John 3:1, 1 John 4:9-11 and Psalm 89:1-2.
47 Jeremiah 29:11-13 and Romans 8:28.

Chapter 12
Doing What It Takes

I fervently hoped for my sponsored US-based job. I felt that God would definitely come through at the last minute. I was calmer in my mind and in my spirit. I used my prayer jar to store my written prayers. The act of putting my prayers in the jar was synonymous to leaving them at the foot of Jesus' cross. However, I did take them up again as I worried, and then I put them down at the cross again. I began a cycle of worry-and-hope, but I was no longer psychotic.

I still prayed and fasted. I still listened to my Nigerian gospel music and I even went back to listening my Jamaican gospel and other favorites. I mellowed out a bit and the neighbors stopped glaring at me because they could now sleep. However they resumed their aborted whispers whenever I stepped outside.

I continued to attend that local church. But I still kept them in the outer court[48] of my life. A few of them knew that my call center job had folded, but none knew of my limit to remain in the USA. I became somewhat close to one family, because they had adopted a bi-racial three-year-old girl. I taught the mother how to care for and manage the little girl's hair. I visited their home once for a barbecue and they made me feel welcome. However when you don't feel good about yourself, then you can't really make friends. In retrospect, it wasn't that those persons were unkind - they did try to befriend me. But I kept pulling away because I didn't like what I had become. I was not living up to my expectations. I was ashamed of myself and I became a recluse by choice.

By this time, my online tutoring job also ended. I was no longer under-employed, I was just plain-old unemployed! I used to be comforted by money coming into my hands. When I was not earning, I became uneasy. I didn't become psychotic again, but I was uneasy. I began to embrace unswerving faith in Jesus Christ.

My car developed mechanical problems, and it was also time to renew its documents. I couldn't risk driving around

---

48 In the Old Testament, there were different levels of proximity to the sanctuary where the Ark of God resided. There were the outer court, the inner court, and then the Holy of Holies (contained within the sanctuary).

with expired car documents and get into trouble with the police. I have always been keen to keep all interactions with law enforcement officials to a minimum.

I went to one mechanic who quoted me a figure that would totally wipe out my savings. It was not an option for me to pay that much. I needed my car because I no longer lived along a bus route, and I still had vital grocery and laundry runs to make.

One day as I was driving along the main highway home, the Holy Spirit prompted me to turn onto an unfamiliar road, but I didn't. Afterwards I kept having a distinct impression that I would find a mechanic along that road. The next time I was driving to the Walmart in Vestal, I got the same prompt again. I turned onto that road and soon I saw a small mechanic store. I drove into their parking lot, but they were closed.

I returned the following Monday. The business was a small family-owned operation with the head mechanic being the owner and adherent of good old-fashioned honesty and uprightness. When they came back with the estimate of what it would take to make my car road worthy, I was astonished. The estimate was under US$400! The previous mechanic I visited wanted to charge me around US$4000! I was very happy and of course, I arranged to get my car fixed. The car passed inspection and I got my documents for the car renewed! Hallelujah!

I shared this testimony at the church. I may have kept my affairs private, but I wanted to share that glimmer of hope to encourage another. This matter pushed me into more faith-based actions. I wrote statements of affirmation regarding a full-time sponsored US job and put them all over my apartment. I did all I could to keep my hopes up.

My funds dwindled as the end of my OPT drew nearer. There were not only no interviews, but the possible jobs to which I could apply dried up too. But I kept believing those affirmations pasted all over my studio. I believed even when my US savings completely dried up. I still believed even when I withdrew my very last funds from my account in Jamaica. I felt that God just had to come through for me in these last, desperate and frantic moments.

I started to sell my possessions: a small TV, a microwave, books, bags, pots, a plate set, etc. Getting rid of my book collection was difficult. I loved those books, but the ones that I could not sell; I donated to the Vestal Library. At least some other persons would be able to enjoy them. I suffered through donating certain items of my mother's clothing that I had been keeping as memorabilia. I painlessly donated my own coats, clothes and boots. I tried to sell my second-hand furniture that was in storage, but no one was interested.

I became strapped for food money, so I began to fast by force. I even had to ask my elder sister Jewell in Jamaica if she could assist me to pay my rent in the USA! My only surviving elder brother Robert now lived in the USA, and he sent me US$115 on the day my rent was due. I collected that money from the MoneyGram outlet in Endicott and I went straight to the Resident Manager to pay for one week of accommodation. I had no more money to pay for any additional weeks.

I still had internet - I had to keep submitting job applications. I began watching YouTube videos on the tiny house movement, alternate living, people living full-time in RVs, etc. I paid closer attention to the videos made by people living in their cars. I noted how to keep myself clean while living full-time in a vehicle, meal arrangement and how to keep occupied and out of the car in daylight hours. Most importantly, I learned about places to park a vehicle to sleep for the night. The Holy Spirit was prepping me for my lowest and darkest point yet.

Afterthoughts

It can be so hard to break away from our own plans for our lives and to accept the blueprint that Christ has for us. I felt that Jesus would work it out for me to legally remain in the US. I was still pursuing my own will. I didn't even think to ask Jesus for details about His plans for my life. I feared that what I so desperately wanted was not in His plans for me. It was a combination of fear that I wouldn't like His plans, and arrogance that my way was better. I now know better and I have since repented of this mentality.

Beloved, you don't have to fear that Jesus is going to lead you to some place where His love, mercy, provision and protection can't keep you. No, we can't come up with a better set of plans than Jesus. Why? Well, we don't have His power, or His perspective.[49] Trust and believe that wherever Jesus leads you, and whatever He sets you to do, it will all work out for your greater good and to His utmost glory.[50]

---

49 Psalm 147:5, Isaiah 40:28-31 and Isaiah 55:8-13.
50 Jeremiah 29:11, Isaiah 43:1-2, 11, 18-19 and Romans 8:28.

Chapter 13
Homeless

I became homeless: in spite of all my degrees, fasting, prayers, faith-affirming posters and declarations. Although the studio was not the best accommodation, it was still a roof over my head, four solid walls and a floor beneath. I wouldn't even have that now.

I realized by the Tuesday of that last week that I would need to live in my car. The Hyundai Santa Fe had enough space. By Thursday I had all my bags packed for that move. On the Friday, I told the landlord and resident manager that I had a family emergency and would leave the next morning. Did I lie? Yes. Why did I lie? I didn't want them to bar me from leaving. I was supposed to give two weeks' notice. But I had no way of knowing that I would become homeless by force. It's not my finest moment. Yes, I have since repented for that lie. If said persons read this chapter, I'm sorry for lying to you.

I moved all my belongings into my car by 4:00 AM that Saturday. I didn't want any spectators. I was an expert at swiftly closing chapters and eradicating all traces of myself from physical spaces. I told the inhabitants of that motel goodbye, jumped into my car and drove off like I had some destination in mind.

My car had too much stuff, and I had to create some space to sleep. I parked in the furthest corner of the local Union Center supermarket parking lot. I sorted through my stuff and selected more items for donations. I would need to do more before nightfall, but I was exhausted.

I sat in Barnes and Noble to while away my first day of homelessness. My dinner, from Walmart, was the smallest serving of General Tso's chicken and fried potato wedges. I had my gallon bottle of water filled, as well as my bathroom pee-jar and lined bucket in place. I rigged the backseat of my SUV with some red black-out curtains. I also fashioned some DIY window shades from black plastic bags. These bags would roll up above the windows and the curtains pulled to the sides during daylight hours.

I did my final donations that evening, to create a bed space. My life was all about shedding my possessions, regardless of how I felt about those items. I thought of nothing but survival. I was numb; crying was an expense that I couldn't afford.

It was still a lively Saturday night of shopping at the Vestal Walmart, so I couldn't select a spot to sleep as yet. I went back to Barnes and Noble to wait for their 10:00 PM closing. I brushed my teeth covertly in the front seat of my SUV in the deserted Barnes and Noble parking lot. I didn't want anyone to see me, as that would be a dead giveaway that I was a car-dweller. I opened my car door slightly to spit the water on the ground and to rinse my toothbrush with my small water bottle.

Eventually the Walmart activity reduced around midnight. I drove across their parking lot to a space far away from the entrance, but under one of their lights. I parked and rolled the front windows almost to a close. I then crab-crawled into the backseat, and made sure that all was dark and private from any peeping Toms. I did a series of gymnastic moves to perform my evening wash and put on my nightwear. I then tried to settle down to sleep. I could only sit down in one corner of the backseat and lean sideways to rest my head and upper body on some bags which I had covered with a towel. I then covered myself with a sheet from my feet to my neck. For the rest of my time as a car-dweller, I struggled with persistent side pain.

I was so nervous that first night of sleeping in my car. I was worried that I would be discovered and chased out in the middle of the night. I didn't see any notices prohibiting overnight parking, but I was still skittish. The first three nights were very difficult. One night I tensed when I heard a car park close to mine and two men got out to go start their shift at Walmart. I was often jolted awake by the sound of the parking lot sweeper cleaning the area around my car. Occasionally, someone would try to peek inside my car. But I was locked up tight and secure, with my car alarm activated, and all my personal privacy settings in place. I soon got accustomed to the sweepers and their antics. If anything, they became my alarm clock. I would wake up in order to complete my morning wash and dress, so that I would look presentable for the day ahead.

I used Walmart's bathrooms for waste removal and cleaning. I also went into the store to buy breakfast items. I would then drive away from my sleeping lot to another more secluded and quieter spot where I would have my morning breakfast. Then I would drive up to Target's parking lot and sit quietly in the front seat, watching the morning come alive as people drove along the Vestal highway below. Then I'd drive back to Barnes and Noble for the day, where I could speed-read a book, or more likely use their internet to watch YouTube videos to distract myself from the aimless nature of my life.

I worried that people would discover my homelessness. I took great pains to make sure that I looked clean and smelled right. It was difficult to keep clean in a small space. I was sure to smile and be cordial, as I was now becoming quite a fixture in Barnes and Noble's small lounge area. I was constantly aware that I did not have the customary Starbuck's cup and a plate of something delicious before me.

I was embarrassed to visit my car in the daytime. Persons would glance in the backseat windows at my cluttered interior. Most would walk away with a shrug and a not-my-business attitude. But for a few others, it would click. They would give me a brief look of pity as they walked away to help preserve whatever shreds of dignity I had left. I felt like the worst of the worse. My education and all my efforts to live a better life were all worthless and useless.

I continued in my homeless routine for two full weeks: from August 27 to September 11, 2016. Initially I told no one - except my elder sister, Jewell and her oldest daughter, Sanya (who were in Jamaica) - that I was homeless and living in my car. They were understandably worried. I eventually told my old high school friend Taniesha, and my SUNY Binghamton friend Sherryllene about my situation. Taniesha helped me with some funds which I used to eat and survive, and Sherryllene paid for my one-way ticket to Jamaica on September 12, 2016. I will always be grateful to my siblings and these two ladies for being there for me during my darkest hours. I pray that God will continue to bless and keep them all.

I had failed to successfully immigrate as expected. I believed that I had lost my opportunity to make something better of my life. I was Dr. Sophia C. Terrelonge, but I had failed. I would return to Jamaica of my own accord, but I would return with nothing of worth; no money or resources. I felt like a deportee, but without the legal ramifications of that status. I was ready to say goodbye and end my chapter of living in the USA. I was completely worn out and desolate.

Afterthoughts

I wish that someone had told me that one episode of failure does not equate to a failed life. I wish that I knew that God's blessings are independent of geographical location and human actions. Beloved, you know now. Your life is not the sum total of your failures, there is more to you than that.

There are two things that you need in the wake of any major upheaval in your life: God's forgiveness and you forgiving yourself. I believe that once we have a changed mind regarding our past and the necessary forgiveness, then we can begin to move forward. When our "perfectly manufactured" lives are demolished by the fire of trials, scorched earth remains. This scorched earth gives us the opportunity for a fresh start, and the ability to build again. But this time, we must be sure to build in keeping with Jesus' divine and bespoke blueprints for our lives.[51]

---

51 Matthew 11:28-30 and Psalm 116:7.

Chapter 14

This is the End: Goodbye and Hello

I was maniacally busy on my last day of homelessness. I wanted to surrender my car, but the finance company kept delaying the pick-up! I had to ask a good church brother and his wife, to hold on to it until the company would pick it up. They were surprised to know that I lived in it and they were kind enough to agree to keep it for me.

I booked a hotel room in Johnson City around 1:00 PM on September 11, 2016. I lugged all my bags into the room and began to shed my most prized possessions. I separated them into two piles. There was a large one for the last donation drop. The second smaller one was destined to follow me into the unknown in Jamaica. I packed my bags and locked them, and took the donations into the car. I locked the hotel room and drove off for the last time in the USA. I drove away in tears; feeling like God had pushed me into an abyss and stomped on my soul. I was nothing.

My life was pointless and a complete waste.

I dropped off my donations, left the car at my friends' home, and then the husband of that family drove me back to the hotel afterwards. As much as he was speaking words of encouragement to me on the way back, I just could not feel them. I could hear them, but my soul was dead anyways. I knew that God was there, but I ceased to believe that He was benevolent to me.

I got back into my room exhausted. I ate the last Walmart meal that characterized my homelessness. I should have enjoyed that hotel bed after two weeks of sleeping on the backseat of the car, but I didn't. I was riddled with worry about what would happen once I got home. How quickly would I get work? How would I deal with having zero personal space as an adult in someone else's house? I was just very depressed.

I went to bed around 12:00 AM and woke up again at 2:00 AM to get ready. I was determined to make my final flight. I got myself ready, double-checked my bags, called a cab and waited. Within ten minutes the cab was there. After I ditched more of my things in the garbage (to be at the correct weight), and checked my bags in at the ticket counter, I went through security. I sat waiting for my 5:55 AM flight to begin boarding. I just wanted to get on and not think too much about it.

I flew from Binghamton to Philadelphia, and then from Philadelphia to Montego-Bay, Jamaica. During the stopover of almost 3 hours in Philadelphia, I bitterly reflected on my first US job market search in that city. Now Philadelphia would be my final US city before I returned home, penniless and in disgrace. I said goodbye to my former dreams in the USA and said hello to my uncertain life in my homeland.

I was a voluntary deportee, returning to my country with no resources. However, unlike a deportee, I would be able to visit the USA again with a B1/B2 (business/tourism) visa. I was gutted, but relieved. I didn't want to become an illegal immigrant. I had zero desire to live a life fearing the Immigration and Customs Enforcement (ICE). I wanted to be free - even if it meant earning the lower Jamaican wages.

I got into Jamaica on September 12, 2016 at 12:45 PM. Many of the people on my flight were all bubbly and happy. Their holiday in my country was beginning and they were giddy with anticipation. I was deeply depressed. My elder sister Jewell had agreed to shelter me until I found a job. She had also agreed to pick me up from the Donald Sangster International Airport in Montego-Bay and transport me to her home.

When I cleared immigration, I collected my bags. I had two large bags and a carry-on suitcase, so I had to explain to customs that I was returning home after studying abroad. The lady at the declaration counter had to ask me why I was coming back home to Jamaica. Why didn't I "run-off"[52] in America? She then called over her friend to "witness" the unusual case of a Jamaican returning voluntarily from the USA after living there! Their unprofessionalism was embarrassing. However, I remained polite so that I could leave the airport without being harassed with fees that I couldn't pay.

I got outside and looked for somewhere to sit, all the while witnessing the happy family reunions and holiday-goers leaving the airport. I had no phone to call my sister, but she knew what time I would arrive. Soon I was the only one from my flight still waiting with my bags. I bought a Jamaican patty and a soda because I was so hungry. I sat and waited. Eventually workers in the lounge area began to ask if anyone was coming for me. I told them that my sister had agreed to pick me up.

I then had to answer the next question of where my sister was coming from (she was coming from _____, St. Ann). Then I heard that wasn't so far from the airport.

_____

52 To "run off" means to refuse to leave a country after entering it for a short-term visit.

They asked why didn't I just hire a car and go there on my own? And so I explained that I was coming home without any money since I couldn't get a job in the USA. They replied with looks of disbelief and shock. How can there be no jobs in the mighty USA? What? How was this possible in the land of milk and honey? Where money was just growing on trees? Why didn't I marry a US citizen and get my "stay"?[53] I smiled at these queries and gave no further replies. A cleaning lady lent me her phone to call my sister, who told me they were on the way.

I waited... and waited, nearly 5 hours. It was a fairly pleasant day, except that it was raining heavily, and the lounge area only had a roof and no walls. I watched people from several other flights - that came after my own - exit the customs section and get picked up. I felt unwanted and unloved.

I began to feel like my sister didn't really want me in her home and so didn't care to pick me up on time. But it turned out that they left home late. Then my brother-in-law's truck broke down on the way and they had to get assistance to resume the journey. But I didn't know that at the time and I just felt alone. I was abandoned by everybody. I blamed God for my predicament of being

---

53 This word "stay", when used in the immigration context, means green card and/or citizenship.

entirely dependent and a burden on everyone.

Eventually, they arrived and we drove from Montego Bay to my sister's home. Naturally they wanted to know how I navigated life without a roof, a floor and four walls. I obliged them. I recounted the "thrills" of living in a car - since no one in my family had ever been homeless. We caught up on news and so forth. I assured them that I would get a job ASAP. Then they would have their space again, and of course I would re-pay them.

I never thought that when I left for the USA in 2009 that I would return in such a penniless and broken way seven years later. My hopes were extinguished, my dreams were assassinated. I felt nothing; I was just a shell of myself. I would now have the strain of communicating with many persons in the socially-appropriate ways. I was a depressed introvert who would have to live with two older adults, a special needs young adult and a teenager. While I loved them, I was dreading this prospect. I just wanted to curl up in a dark place in solitude. But alas! I would be forced to pretend to be a normal human being with extroverted tendencies. This made me even more depressed.

Afterthoughts

When we undergo traumatic situations, we often want to hide ourselves. We seek a safe haven of solitude. At the time, I was deprived of physical solitude. I had lost all connection with Jesus Christ. I was adrift in an ocean of nothingness.

Let's pray:

> *Lord Jesus, even when we think that we have nothing, let us remember Your gift of life. With life, we have a hope in You that assures us all will be well. Your Word says that there is hope for a tree that although it is cut down, it will sprout again and its branches will live. Even though this tree's root dies in the ground, the scent of water will make this tree resurrect like a young plant.[54] Lord Jesus, You are the Living Water. Please make the root and the branches of your beloved to live again. Give Your beloved Your unfathomable peace and steadfast trust in You that life will get better. Father, surround us with Your arms of love and grace. We believe that You hear us and that all is already done. We thank You Jesus and we praise You. Amen.*

---

54 Job 14:7-9.

Chapter 15
This is Not Your House!

I was back in my homeland, but I didn't feel at home. This sense of rootlessness was amplified since I was living in someone else's space. I felt out of place in my sister's house. I felt out of place emotionally and spiritually in my own mind and life. I no longer lived, I just existed. I spoke the expected words with no supporting emotions or understanding. There was no "me", because Jesus had left me desolate. So, my "self" was really no one and nowhere. I was just not there. I was a stranger to all – including myself.

Life had further re-defined me to a zero. I was a "has-been" and a "never-was" at the same time. I was a highly educated female, but I never benefitted in any material way from all that education. I felt like a failure. I was not back where I started from, but lower than where I started. When I left Jamaica in 2009, I had my own rented apartment, a car (which was sold) and a sense of promise (although I was mourning my mother's death). Now I was walking and taking taxis everywhere. I had little clothing, and my shelter and food came from someone else. It was humbling and soul-crushing. I completely lost my identity.

My sister's church family was supportive, as they were always praying for me concerning employment. I will always be grateful for their kind words and support. However at the time, I couldn't really receive love or attention. I went through the motions with everything and everyone. I was apathetic; I couldn't even bother to care.

My job search started the week of my return. My laptop died that same week - talk about trials! I borrowed my teenage niece's notebook to send applications while she was away at school. I hated this dependency.

This was not my home and I felt caged. I felt caged by their family routines and dynamics. I felt caged by their expectations of how I would operate in *their* home. There were minor conflicts from the varied personalities. I was a square peg that couldn't fit in the round hole. I helped with the household duties (which I didn't mind) since I couldn't make monetary contributions.

My growing depression and taciturn nature meant that I could be seen, but I was mentally and emotionally unavailable. This made it difficult for everyone around me. Unfortunately, mental issues are not understood (or tolerated) in the general Jamaican population. And so it was a problematic situation.

I kept submitting applications and praying that one would lead to a job, any job. I even applied to the dreaded call center jobs that just required CSECs and GCEs.[55] I was scraping the proverbial bottom of the barrel. Since I was in St. Ann, a nature tourism hub, I also applied to hotels and businesses in Ocho Rios. I would get the odd interview, where they would tell me I was too qualified. I considered deleting my degrees, but I could not locate evidence of my CSEC and GCE passes. I would also have to lie about my work experience. Every job I had worked to date hinted at my higher level of education. I also didn't want to lie on my applications.

I remember one particular interview. The post was for a store clerk in a mobile phone franchise in Ocho Rios. The store attendants were kind, as I waited with a few other 20+ year-old candidates for the interviews to begin.

Two hours later, the store manager (a lady in her fifties), called me in to a dark, claustrophobic back "office" of which she was clearly proud. Although I had submitted my electronic CV, she asked me to write down my qualifications on a sheet of paper. She then rudely interrogated me about why I wanted to work as a store clerk with all my degrees.

---

55 CSECs and GCEs are the Caribbean's equivalent of a GED in the USA or a high school diploma.

Why didn't I try to stay in America? Why would I even think to return to Jamaica where there were no jobs?

Her attitude was nasty and cranky. She took a clear pleasure in talking down to me. She then asked for my passport-sized photo and told me to write my name on the back of it. Afterwards she had the gall to tell me that I was over-qualified for the position and that I wasn't likely to be hired. I cordially bid her goodbye, shook her hand and left that dungeon.

I smiled and waved goodbye at the store attendants. I blindly walked around Ocho Rios, as the usual afternoon rains descended, pushing me further into depression. I had served Jesus faithfully and I felt that He was failing me in a grand way!

I bitterly mused: "Look at what just happened with that woman! Jesus, what did I do to You? Why are You punishing me? If I did something wrong, please tell me so that I can fix it and move on with my life!"

After the fiasco at the Ocho Rios store, I was soon asked to interview with a lady who owned a booth at a local natural attraction. She was way younger than I was. Her skin and hair glowed with youth and privilege, and her accent indicated frequent trips abroad. I was being interviewed for a part-time job manning her shoe rental and plastic wares booth. She also inquired why a Ph.D. trained in the

USA would return to unemployment in Jamaica. But since she was from an "old money" background, her inquisition was genteel. It was so subtle that I only noticed it after the interview ended. I was suddenly quite annoyed with her and her privilege! She had said that I would soon get a job matching my education and leave her employ. I heard nothing from her again.

I then had two interviews in Montego-Bay. The first was at a call center. Again, the interviewer expressed surprise that I would apply for such a lowly job as a customer service representative. I was asked about my desired hourly salary. I forgot what I said, but the interviewer sadly shook her head. I would not get paid anywhere near that amount. I was shocked, because I didn't think it was a high number. She was in her early forties, but she was kind to encourage me to wait for a job that matched my educational background.

The second interview required going to another call center for some tests. I got a two-week notice about the nature of these tests, so I had time to practice. This post supported an accountancy firm, so I reviewed my basic book-keeping topics. There would also be general reasoning and typing-speed tests. I travelled again from the hills of St. Ann to Montego-Bay on the test day. However, the traffic made me arrive about twenty minutes late. I rushed through each test, and finished with the typing-speed one at the end. I failed! I typed six words less than required! I was gutted! I felt like I wasted my sister's money to travel to Montego-Bay that day. Of course, I heard nothing from that company again.

I felt like I was nothing and nobody. I was in my homeland, but I was not welcome. Everywhere I went, I was asked why I returned home. It was a big taboo: a Ph.D. holder returning from the USA to unemployment and deprivation in Jamaica. I returned to Jamaica with no money. I had no house built anywhere. I had no business in place. I was an alien in my Jamaica, which seemed to no longer have a place for me. I was a stranger, a sojourner who could find no place to rest. I did not feel welcome in my country.

I could see the cobwebs continually growing on the seat that Jesus once occupied in my heart. I prayed out of habit, not expecting Him to answer any of my requests. I "worshipped" in my sister's church, but not out of any real reverence. I knew how to do the motions, since I knew all about church life and its mannerisms. I felt abandoned. They would often say that "God is good", but I couldn't honestly say that "God is good" in the customary reply. As far as I could see, He was not being good to me. It seemed like Jesus was nowhere to be found.

Afterthoughts

We are creatures of habit. We like to follow set routines and we enjoy stability in our lives. We tend to fear change, because at our core, we want everything to remain the same. So when life goes haywire, and we lose our identities and it's very traumatic. These identities were often formed by, and hinged on external factors: our education, our jobs, our financial and social standing, etc. All that defined you has left, taking your sense of self as well.

However, to truly follow Jesus Christ, all self must be crucified. It has to die. We will feel extreme pain as our "manufactured" selves die. Death is painful. Death is traumatic. However this change is necessary for true growth in Christ.[56] I just feel led to pray:

> *Father, help Your beloved ones to let go of these "manufactured" selves. Jesus, please grant them the peace to trust Your breaking and molding processes. Give them hope and comfort at this time. Please let them find You as a true Father and Friend, who loves them. I thank You in advance for making them as new honorable vessels for their good and Your continual glory. I trust You to complete the great work that You have started in them. I thank You Jesus. Amen.*

56 Galatians 2:20.

Beloved, do not fear your seasons of change. You have to change internally to manage the changes that surround you externally. Trust Christ throughout each change that you experience. Without faith in Jesus Christ, we can't please Him, because we will never trust Him to lead us. We can't rely on our perceptions and subjective value systems to be successful on this journey.[57] We have to walk by faith and not by sight.[58] You will eventually see that these changes, these upheavals all serve to move you closer to your divinely appointed destiny. So, walk in the faith and strength needed for your unique journey to the center of God's perfect will for you.

---

57 Proverbs 3:5-6.
58 Hebrews 11:1 and 6, and 2 Corinthians 5:7.

Chapter 16
Finding Him Again

I began to feel differently in early November 2016. I experienced the usual renewed bereavement on November 1st, which was my mother's birthday. But I didn't sink into greater depression as I expected. Nothing had changed in the physical dimension. I was still unemployed and an unwilling dependent.

I began to feel a glimmer of change within my own heart. A sense of pragmatism first came. I was in Jamaica, and I couldn't change that. I had no means to live elsewhere, so I needed to make the best of that situation. I became a bit more "present" in my human interactions. I started to feel little more hopeful in my continuous job applications. I was thawing out, bit by bit.

Then I began to hear Him again. Was it Him though, or was it me? I had moments of doubt that I could now hear Jesus again. Then as my soul continued to thaw, I began to feel like myself again. The more my heart came alive, the more clearly I could hear His voice... again.

I thought that I would never be a dedicated Christian again. But I am grateful that Jesus had not really abandoned me. I just thought He wasn't there because life wasn't going according to my script. Life had gone haywire and I felt alone. However, Jesus assured me that He was always there. He began to show me instances where He was with me during my struggles in the USA and in my homeland. I thought Jesus had left me, but He was still there. Thank you, Daddy Jesus for being present, always!

It took some time for me to rebuild my spiritual muscles. I started to read my You-Version Bible plans again. I started to pray again - it felt like I was actually having conversations with Jesus once more. I began to fast again, but this time for spiritual strength instead of the material. Everything was: *again.* Renewed. Refreshed. Revived. Round 2.

I would still "zone out", but it was to spend time with Jesus. I began to see people and things from His perspective. I received His wisdom about what I should say and how I should act in different circumstances. Jesus also revealed the areas in which I needed to change in order to progress. I felt both relief and joy that I was not forgotten. I was undergoing a vital phase to build my faith and ground my character in Christ.

As my internal life changed, it slowly reflected in my external life and my interactions with others. I no longer worshipped mechanically at my sister's church. I felt alive as I worshipped in spirit and in truth.[59] A change was coming, but it had to start within me first.

I continued to submit job applications. I got an interview for a sales/administrative position in an Ocho Rios boutique hotel. I first had to submit a short article marketing the hotel's experience to its guests. This was a major challenge, as I had not written anything creative since 2015. However, I prayed about it and Jesus provided the insight and words that flowed just right. I shared it with my sister and nieces (to their approval), and then submitted the article to the hotel and prepared for my interview.

I was optimistic about this interview. Even if I didn't get this job, I was still determined to do my best and maintain a positive outlook. I arrived early to the interview and was asked to sit in the hotel's general waiting area. This was one of the longstanding vintage-designed hotels. The guests were mainly Americans, 50 years and above, who always vacationed in Jamaica and always stayed at the hotel, even in select rooms. It was an expensive luxury hotel, where rooms went in excess of US$500 per night! I

---

59 John 4:23.

was pleasant to the guests in the waiting area and had brief conversations with a few. I wasn't doing this for show, but because I genuinely liked the place and the atmosphere.

I can still see the expansive blue Caribbean Sea glimmering and rippling under the morning sun. I couldn't keep my eyes away from the beautiful seascape that unfolded from the main veranda of the waiting area. I reflected that most of my fellow Jamaicans were unaware of the incredible beauty of our country. Most of these spaces were inaccessible to many, and would unfortunately remain so. The tourists were all tanned, rested and satisfied with their vacation. The workers seemed happy as they moved about briskly to their tasks to keep the wealthy clientele satisfied. It seemed like a good place to work.

I was called in for my interview after an hour and half - I didn't mind waiting though! I entered a large conference room decorated with international antiques. The two female interviewers were roughly around my age. They shone with contentment and financial wellbeing. There was little interest in me being a Ph.D. from the USA and seeking Jamaican employment. They did ask if I was sure that I wanted to work in sales, as my previous positions were not in that field. I expressed my openness to a new career path and outlined my transferable skills.

I pretended to have a telephone conversation with one of their guests calling from overseas. I drew on my call center experience and delivered. I answered other job-specific questions, and received info about the timeline of their recruitment process. The interview ended and I bid them goodbye. As I walked off the property along its tree-lined walkway, I was in a positive, upbeat mood. Even if I didn't get the position, I had done my best.

Alas, I heard nothing from them, but I didn't mind. I still felt that I would get a job - I just needed to wait patiently. I was happy to know that Jesus was still around and that He still loved me. Jesus had not abandoned me, He was there all along. And that was what mattered most of all!

Afterthoughts

We tend to lament beside the doors Jesus closed. Beloved, wipe your tears. He closed those doors for reasons we may never know. Get up from your lamentations! Shake off the gloominess! Shake off the faithlessness!

Ask Jesus to show you the next open door that is waiting for you. Once Jesus shows you this door, ask Him about His timing for you to enter into your "next". I invite you to walk through each new open door with confidence. Know that Jesus Christ has already gone before you to make all preparations for your arrival. Forget about your past.

Release it all by His grace and strength. Ask Jesus Christ for the wisdom and fortitude to successfully complete your next chapter of life. Beloved, walk right in to your next phase by faith in Christ alone!

Chapter 17
Learning to Live Again

My personal resurrection stretched from November into December 2016. I was more in tune with Jesus Christ. It was like getting re-acquainted with a friend I hadn't seen in many years. There were moments of fond recollection, as I recalled His past faithfulness. The Holy Spirit also reminded me of certain impactful sermons. I was learning how to live the second phase of my life with Jesus Christ.

I made gradual progress in my social life. I was nicer to my family and I even began to make more friends at my sister's church. I now exuded more human warmth and kindness. It was like I had come out of a coma and was experiencing life again.

The Lord physically woke me up one pre-dawn morning and told me to make work skirts. I replied in thought: "What? Make work skirts? Jesus, I don't know how to sew clothes! I don't have a sewing machine! Sew them by hand?" This instruction persisted all of that day.

I had no money to buy any cloth and sewing supplies, so I was at a loss. However, God began to use persons from my sister's church and a few old friends to give me pocket money. I saved as much as possible after accounting for my feminine needs. These persons may have thought that it wasn't much, but I was grateful. The Lord was working here! Soon I got started on this little venture.

I bought cloth in 1.5 to 2 yards increments in black, purple, red and a floral print. I also purchased a pair of scissors, and other seamstress items. My mother had ensured that I would always have a decent stock of needles and thread on hand. In my youth I mended my few pieces of clothing multiple times to make them last.

Jesus showed me how to take my measurements and how to cut my cloth. I sewed all the skirts by hand. The average was a simple skirt every week and a half, as I only sewed while I was home alone with my special needs niece. No one else knew of my crazy adventure into clothes design and creation! I just wanted to obey Jesus and I found that I liked creating these simple pieces. I even wore a few of these skirts to church with my sister - that was when she found out.

Yes, the job application factory continued to churn out mass production each week. But I now did so with hope and purpose. I just wanted to be in position to capitalize on any opportunity. I saw my job search through new eyes. This placement would be in accordance with God's will and His divine purpose for my life.

I came across an interesting vacancy for a student affairs managerial post at a local private university. I had always worked in academia teaching students. I didn't know about the administrative dimension in higher education and I wanted to see what it was like. So, I applied, but this application was unique. At that time, my sister's internet was down, and so I visited a cyber store to check if all was well in my e-world. It was there that I saw that advertisement. It was also in that same store that I submitted that application.

I got an interview. Nice! However, the main campus was in Kingston. They wanted to interview me in the morning, but it would have been a nightmare for me to get into Kingston on time. Eventually I was able to get a 2:30 PM interview instead. I excitedly told my sister about this new interview, and arranged to stay with my niece Sanya and her family for the trip.

The journey into Kingston that morning was quite eventful. First, I had trouble getting a bus that was "ready" to go to the capital from the Ocho Rios terminal. For my non-Jamaican readers, "ready" buses are privately owned and are packed past maximum capacity before they begin each trip. All I could see that morning on the Kingston queue were empty buses. The Holy Spirit led me to return to the bus terminal's gates where I saw a standing-room-only bus ready to go into Kingston. I hopped on and began the torturous standing commute. I stood for nearly the entire 2.5-hour drive into Kingston that day. It was my first time standing in a bus for such a long drive since my return to Jamaica.

It was quite a shock, as I re-learned how to "balance" myself with the turns and bumps of the roadway. In Jamaica it's unacceptable to lean on someone else while standing in a crowded bus/vehicle - even if you're standing on only one leg! Even in a seated position, no leaning is allowed! As an adult, you are expected to monitor your body parts at all times. Never encroach on another's valuable real estate on any public transportation. Your first infraction will get you a nasty stare (which your apology and physical realignment should lessen). But if you had leaned on someone too hard, you would be pushed into your "spot" and you may also receive some Jamaican expletives. Thus was the state of affairs that morning.

I reached the emerging bustle of downtown Kingston around 11:30 AM. I quickly caught further public transport to my niece's apartment, where her husband let me in. I showered away the funk of the stressful morning commute and prepared for my interview.

I was about 30 minutes early to the venue. I was called in 45 minutes later to a panel of three ladies who were key personnel at the institution. I was on familiar ground: academia again! They weren't interested in why a US graduate was job hunting in Jamaica, they wanted to know my start date. I said that I would be able to start ASAP. The interview ended on a positive note and I returned to my niece's place. The next morning, I returned to St. Ann.

I wasn't even worried about whether or not this job would call me again. If something didn't happen -in spite of my best efforts- then it wasn't in the will of God for me. I was not my usual worried self. I began to experience and enjoy Jesus' unfathomable peace and communion. I was alive again!

Afterthoughts

What a difference a change in perspective makes! I viewed my past jobs as merely fulfilling my financial and esteem needs. I had different rooms within my life. Some were labelled salvation and spiritual matters. Other rooms were labelled personal goals and creative output. There were rooms for family and friends. Another set of rooms were labelled career and financial wellbeing. I thought of myself as the only common factor across these rooms.

However, I was wrong and I had to repent of this mindset. Beloved, Jesus Christ must be welcomed in all of these rooms. If we are to experience true peace and alignment with the will of Christ, then He must be the common factor across all areas of our lives.

Psalm 37:4 reads:

> *"Delight yourself also in the Lord, and He shall give you the desires of your heart."*

I used to think of this scripture in a transactional sense: If I serve God really well, then He will just bless whatever I do - as long as I'm not hurting anybody. But I have learned that this is not what this scripture means at all! As I grow closer to Christ in all my ways, then my heart's desires will be molded and aligned with His divine will for my life. When I am in correct alignment with Jesus Christ, then my regenerated desires coincide with His will. It is only then that He grants me those desires.

We often sing songs about surrendering to Jesus. However do we really mean what we sing? Do we comprehend what surrendering to Jesus really looks like? Surrendering to Jesus' will for our lives means actively following His blueprint. And guess what? We each have our unique, divinely inspired blueprint. So we cannot look at each other's lives to figure out our own blueprint. Each person must seek Christ and spend quality time with Him, to discover His specially designed blueprint for him/her.

A life spent in ignorance of your divine purpose is a wasted one. It doesn't matter how much wealth you acquire and how many accolades you get: you will feel empty and unfulfilled. When you discover your purpose, when you unearth the reason you greet each morning alive and mentally aware: you will find true fulfilment. This awesome sense of fulfilment comes from following your specific blueprint. The only way to get your own blueprint is by a life truly surrendered to Jesus Christ.

I'll be honest: surrendering to Jesus Christ is hard. We always want to be in control. As mere mortals we cannot see things from an eternal perspective. We can only see a snapshot called "Now" and some other pictures in an album called "Then". But Jesus Christ can see the entire continuum of our lives from beginning to end. Therefore, He has the best perspective to draw all the blueprints for our lives.

Beloved, what are you holding back from Christ? A partial surrender is no surrender. I can assure you that your current circumstances are not permanent. I believe that Jesus Christ can change any situation. My dear, draw near to Jesus, surrender all that you are to Him. Come and hear what He has to tell you of His plans for your life. Your true fulfilment awaits you in the company of Jesus Christ.

Chapter 18

Daring to Dream Again and Flying Free!

In December 2016, I was much nicer to be around. I had a feeling that all would work out well and something new would happen in the job dimension. But I didn't know exactly where and when it would emerge. I was waiting with happy expectation. I was just a better version of myself.

I have a vivid memory of a rain-drenched Sunday morning. This downpour had its genesis in the fat droplets rhythmically striking the zinc roof from 3:00 AM. By 6:00 AM, the rainstorm had unveiled itself, as it furiously lashed everything in its path. No one intended to go to church that day, except for me. I was still getting ready for the service, even when the rain showed no sign of relenting. However, since my family thought that I'm weird, they just left me to my own devices.

I grabbed my large umbrella and headed onto the verandah. The rain slowed down. I stepped outside to begin my trek to the pick-up point for the church bus. This stop was located downhill from my sister's house. For the first three minutes, it seemed like the rain would completely cease. Then suddenly the heavens opened again, pouring out all its woes upon my umbrella, which leaked through at the top. I felt the steady seep of water onto my scarf-tied head. The violent wind drove the rain under the umbrella, soaking my clothes. The road flooded again, filling my flat shoes with muddied water. I was miserable, but I pressed on to my rendezvous point with the bus.

I picked my way carefully along the last portion of the rough road, trying not to fall in my waterlogged shoes. I was shuddering with cold and beginning to worry about becoming ill. I had no medicine for at-home treatment; talk less of seeing a doctor.

I then heard the Holy Spirit say: "Rejoice evermore! Pray without ceasing!"

As I walked along, I kept hearing Him say: "Rejoice evermore! Pray without ceasing!"

As I waited on the bus, that mantra kept ringing in my mind. I soon forgot about my cold existence. I just focused on those words: "Rejoice evermore! Pray without ceasing!"

As soon as I got into church that morning, I cracked open my Bible. I faintly remembered seeing those words somewhere in the New Testament, but which book? Eventually, He led me to 1 Thessalonians 5:16 and 17:

"Rejoice evermore. Pray without ceasing."

I felt that Jesus was telling me to rejoice and to pray continually, because the end of my current season was near. I also shared the revelation at church during testimony service that day. I was so happy that the Lord would speak directly to me, to assure me that I was not forgotten and to encourage me to persevere.

On December 14, 2016, I got an email stating that I had been awarded the managerial post! Hallelujah! Finally, a job! Glory to God! I was just elated that I would regain my adult independence! I had journeyed through a desert and I now found water to quench my unemployment thirst. I was overjoyed.

I soon came back to reality. The salary was ok - for Jamaica. I tried not to compare it to what I could have earned in the USA. The Holy Spirit reminded me not to despise small beginnings. I was grateful to obtain meaningful paid work. I would be able to have my own home and buy my own food and necessities again. I could also repay my sister for the expenses she incurred on my behalf.

The Sunday following that email was simply divine. I felt like a great weight had been lifted off my shoulders! The "Hallelujah" that I shouted that morning reflected all of that newfound freedom! It came from way down inside me where it had been locked away and I thought that it would never emerge. I then sang (or rather croaked) the chorus of Ada's *Only You Jesus.* I then shared my tearful and somewhat long testimony of homelessness, loss of hope and coming back home to Jamaica unemployed. I am still very grateful and thankful to the pastors and members of my sister's church for their support and prayers. I am also very grateful and wish to thank my sister Jewell, her husband, and my niece Sanya (and her family), and my two younger nieces. I thank you all for being there for me.

I began to plan my transition from dependent to independent living, from St. Ann to Kingston. I would stay with my niece Sanya until I found a place to live on my own. It would be a process of first sleeping on the floor of my new studio apartment atop my niece's borrowed foam mattress. I would cook on a small countertop stove. I would then slowly buy a bed, a refrigerator, and a microwave. It would be frugal living, but it would be living on my own as a productive adult.

My first day of work was great. I was excited and ready to begin work on my portfolio of duties. Within my first work week at that small private university, I met almost all the staff members. I had a good relationship with my immediate supervisor, and I led a small department of three other persons. However, the details of this job and the further oceans Jesus led me to walk upon; I will share - by God's grace - in another book and in short order.

Jesus Christ was never missing from the scene. Jesus was there in the confusion. He was there in the struggle. Jesus was there in the depression. He was there in the lack. Jesus was there in the darkest midnight. I was often so focused on the situation and my feelings that my eyes were blinded to His presence and my ears deafened to His voice. However, I found the quiet assurance that Jesus never abandons us. Jesus is always there, waiting for us to join Him again in communion, and to receive His peace and rest in the midst of it all. I am finally at peace in Him. I am fully resolved to walk each day of my life fully trusting in Christ and surrendering to His perfect will.

Afterthoughts

We often think that Jesus goes missing during our trials, but that's not true. He is omnipresent; He is always there. He is right there in the middle of whatever we have to endure. Jesus Christ does not abandon us. We experience that sense of distance and loss whenever we allow our circumstances to pull us away from earshot. But He never stops pursuing us and speaking life to us. We are the ones who keep pulling away from Him. The love of Jesus Christ for each of us is unconditional and unending. His mercies regenerate with each new sunrise that breaks the horizon.[60] He was always there and He will always be there for us.

Beloved of Christ, I thank you very much for reading this book through to the end. I hope that your heart is blessed and that you are encouraged. I pray that your resolve is strengthened. I want you to know that your story will change for the better, for your good and to His glory.

If you have already made the commitment to serve Jesus Christ wholeheartedly as our Lord and Savior, great! I encourage you to continue to run your Christian race with patience, and further promote the mandate of His Kingdom here on earth.

If you have not yet made the decision to accept Jesus Christ as your Lord and Savior, I invite you to come on board! Jesus Christ made the ultimate sacrifice at Calvary's Cross so that you and I can be reconciled to Him. I invite you to make the conscious decision to follow Jesus Christ, grow in Him, discover your unique blueprint, and fulfill your divine purpose.

---

60 Romans 5:8, John 3:16-17, Psalm 86:15, 1 Chronicles 16:34, Psalm 36:5-10 and Lamentations 3:22-26.

Please join a Bible-believing church in your community, where you can learn more about Jesus Christ and His Word in fellowship with others. It is important for you to be water baptized in Jesus' name and that you receive the fire of His Holy Spirit dwelling inside of you.[61] We cannot walk this Christian journey alone. We need fellow believers in Christ, so that we can encourage each other along the way.

Remember that *Jesus Christ loves you.* You cannot earn His love and you cannot do anything to make Him not love you. His love for you is unending, unconditional and boundless. He thinks the best of you as His beloved child. Jesus Christ has so much in store for you. Go to Him; sit in communion with Him to discover your true purpose. Discover your divine reason for breathing and living each day. Once you find your special "why", use the blueprint that Jesus created just for you, to fulfill your purpose. The Kingdom of Jesus Christ is waiting; the world is waiting, for you to get in alignment. Do all that you can to fulfill your God-appointed purpose in the earth. Be blessed, be encouraged, and be inspired in Jesus' name.

> *Dearly Beloved of Christ, I pray that Jesus' blessings, peace and wisdom be upon you all. Amen.*

---

61 Please read Acts 1 and 2, especially Acts 2:38-39.

Made in United States
North Haven, CT
14 May 2022

19165576R00080